Market
Liberalism

Gordon C. K. Cheung

Market Liberalism

American Foreign Policy Toward China

Transaction Publishers
New Brunswick (U.S.A.) and London (U.K.)

Library of Congress Catalog Number: 98-18320
ISBN: 1-56000-378-2
Printed in the United States of America

Library of Congress Cataloging-in-Publication Data

Cheung, Gordon C. K.
    Market liberalism : American foreign policy toward China / Gordon
C.K. Cheung
        p. cm.
    Includes bibliographical references and index.
    ISBN 1-56000-378-2 (alk. paper)
    1. United States—Foreign economic relations—China. 2. China—
Foreign economic relations—United States. 3. United States—
Economic policy. 4. United States—Foreign relations—China.
5. China—Foreign relations—United States. I. Title.

HF1455.Z4C49   1998
337.73051—dc21   98-18320
                                                                        CIP

Contents

List of Figures and Tables

Preface

U.S.-China relations are a controversial topic by definition. The countries not only represent two of the largest powers in the world but also stand for two different ideologies in world politics. During the cold war, their relations witnessed the change from containment policy to a strategic triangle, and from normalization to rapprochement. There was ongoing military confrontation between the United States and China, first the Korean War and then the Vietnam War. Yet in terms of foreign relations, these terms and analyses, focusing mainly on military and confrontational angles, explain only part of their relations. An important ingredient—market force—deserves much attention if one wants to have a more balanced view of their relations, either during the cold war or the post-cold war period. This is the major objective of this book, to interpret U.S.-China relations by dissecting the facilitation of the market force.

I wish to extend my thanks to Professor C.Y. Chang, who patiently guided me from the pursuit of knowledge to intellectual enrichment. His comments, ideas, and encouragement are invaluable to this study. Professor Wu Guoguang gave useful criticism of my writing, and I am grateful for his concern throughout the writing process. I wish to thank Professor Lee Chin Chuen and Professor John Wong for their time and comments. Susan Blumberg Liu, Barbara Koh, and Dimitri Kaczmarek were enormously helpful in polishing my writing. Many thanks to Irving Louis Horowitz for the publication of my work. The comments made by the anonymous reviewer were particularly useful in refining the argument and shaping the presentation of the thesis in a more readable style. I thank Claudia Kirschhoch for her professional editing.

The University Services Center at the Chinese University of Hong Kong provided sufficient resources on the China materials. Solomon Wong at the United States Information Service in the American Consulate General generously provided updated information about contemporary U.S. politics. In terms of locating firsthand material and the sources for the American side, I benefited from the Eu Tong Sen scholarship, which enabled me to study and conduct research at the University of Hawaii in the latter half of 1995. The East-West Center afforded constant help during my stay in Hawaii. Throughout the research and my academic pursuit, I faithfully extend my gratitude to the Department of Government and Public Administration of the Chinese University of Hong Kong for giving me this opportunity and for their spiritual and financial support as well. I would like to thank the following professors and area specialists who have given me support and insight during different stages of the writing process: Eric Harwit, Hsin Chi Kuan, Reginald Kwok, Oliver Lee, Peter N.S. Lee, Kuang Sheng Liao, Shu Yun Ma, Milan T.W. Sun, King Kwun Tsao, Byron S.J. Weng, and Kui Hung Wong. An early version of chapter 9 in this book was previously published elsewhere. I thank Sage Publications for permission to use "U.S. Policy towards China: Some Theoretical Implications, " *China Report* 32, no. 2 (April-June), pp. 119–132.

Finally, I would like to express my deepest thanks to my wife Flora. Her encouragement and support eased various difficulties during the writing process.

Gordon C.K. Cheung

1

Introduction

*Americans have associated commerce with
open markets, open markets with political
freedom, political freedom with democracy,
and democracy with peace.[1]*
—Jeffrey E. Garten

Reinterpretation of Sino-American Relations

This book attempts to reinterpret U.S. foreign policy toward China after World War II by looking at the externalization of market forces.[2] Throughout the book, I shall put forward the concept of Augmented Market Liberalism (AML) as a theoretical guide to analyze their relations.

AML is defined as a process of assimilation and transformation of a country generated by the externalization effects of the market force. In terms of Sino-American relations, the externalization effects refer to the U.S. construction of a favorable environment to accomplish such change. First, from the foreign policy perspective, the transformation of Japan after 1945 strongly situated the market ingredients and the model of capitalism in the Far East.

The opening up of U.S. domestic markets to Japan and the nurturing of the Japanese market economy gave rise to multiple effects in terms of economic development and marketization toward Asian countries. Second, the success story of the Four Little Dragons further enhanced ideas of using market forces as a linchpin of development. In cold war terminology, these two examples served as the classic cases of the manifestation of containment policy. In the post-cold war era, the denoting effects of U.S. foreign policy are still profound. U.S. interests include: (1) military stability and peace in the Far East; (2) guaranteed economic opportunities in the Far East that cannot be toppled by an abrupt

1

change in the balance—either by the rise of a dominant China or by the internationalization of Japan—of the political environment; and (3) upholding the idea of democracy through economic development in many Asian countries that are adopting a market economy as their development model.

As the major ingredient of U.S. foreign policy toward China, *the pattern of market behavior gave rise to opportunity, enlargement of goals, growth through production and consumption, and the manifest orientation that envisioned change.* The market is a dynamic organ which does not belong to any single country. Yet, it exists within and around countries that contained the ingredients of market forces.

Historically, the transformation effects of the market on a society has long been an academic focal point. Karl Polanyi's groundbreaking book *The Great Transformation* initiated a classic literature studying the anatomy, the pattern of change and the facilitation of change of the market economy in the nineteenth century.[3] The "self-regulating" nature of market behavior actually energized the world toward an astonishing new phase.[4] In addition, as argued by Edward J. Nell, it is "not that market outcomes are *optimal*, [italics in original] but rather that they have a certain objectivity and reflect robust good sense. If you pay attention to the market signals, you ought to do all right; if you don't you will run a serious risk of going under."[5] The momentum of the market and the dynamic forces of liberalism energize the world toward growth in an unprecedented manner. Empirical studies and researches have recently attributed the transformation of the global economy to the market impetus and the force that lies behind it.[6] The post-cold war international economy has witnessed rapid changes in the economic structures of many formerly socialist countries. The demise of the former Soviet Union encouraged the transformation of many centrally planned economies into market-oriented economies. The introduction of private property rights and the vigorousness of market competition are given great attention by many international organizations.[7]

The perpetuation of market forces, in fact, may reconcile Sino-American conflict and disagreement by reorienting their focus on gain through trade instead of through military confrontation. China's government, especially after 1978, gradually internalized the facilitating of market liberalism as an agent of reform.

Fortunately, the market, as an agency of change, performs well in regulating the various transactions involved in Chinese society without excessively violating the political ecology of China. As Susan L. Shirk put it, "the lesson of the Chinese case is that in some varieties of communism, it is possible to move from a command economy to market competition without changing the political rules of the game. Communist rule in and of itself is not an insuperable obstacle to economic transformation."[8] The adaptation to the disciplinary guiding post of market force engendered a model for the change of policy orientation toward internal development as well as foreign investment. In particular, the need for capital and technology caused by China's economic reform and development inevitably leads to further deregulation policy and relaxation. This change is clearly depicted in Margaret M. Peason's study of foreign direct investment (FDI) in China. She strongly emphasized that:

> The growing belief that their [Chinese] economic modernization program required them to absorb foreign capital at even greater levels put them on a course whereby they had to pay attention to foreign concerns, and more generally to ways they might be able to improve the investment environment. Under these conditions, the reformers had little choice but to liberalize.[9]

With respect to U.S.-China relations, U.S. foreign policy assisted in fulfilling these forces. In addition, as China opened to the outside world in the early 1980s, the U.S. needed to implement a policy to incorporate the components of market force. Moreover, the market force, during the post-cold war era, allows the U.S. to maintain world leadership not in such a way as to "command troops and confront enemies" but "to bargain across many different issues and groups, build coalitions, and seize opportunities for agreement."[10] The study of market forces, therefore, enables us to observe the logical sequence and major elements of Sino-American foreign relations since World War II. Before we go to the detail, we must first look back to reveal the historical background.

U.S.-China Foreign Relations in Retrospect

The pendulum of U.S. foreign policy toward China moved from a containment policy at the height of the cold war to an engagement policy in the post-cold war era. In essence, the ideology of American foreign policy has long been embodied in the two concepts of "white man's burden" and "manifest destiny."

"White man's burden" refers to Americans' innate passion for world liberation and the improvement of human conditions. However, such a responsibility, when translated into realistic foreign policy, may sometimes result in a euphemism for expansionism instead of wholehearted altruism.[11] Similarly, "manifest destiny" was a term used to describe the absorption of Texas and the West by Americans in the 1850s. Postwar U.S. policy toward Asia and China is similar, if not identical, to that policy.[12]

Historically, however, U.S. policy toward China, has demonstrated that a lack of mutual respect toward international market forces underlying U.S.-China relations inevitably resulted in setbacks and resentment. The United States had tried to open up China in the late nineteenth century by fostering a foreign policy that was originally aimed at enlarging business opportunities, in contrast to the "sphere-of-influence" policy practiced by other nations.

The first phase of American foreign policy toward China began in the late nineteenth century when the Open Door Notes were promulgated in 1899 and 1900.[13] United States policy was based on its historical orientation toward economic interests and market openness.[14] In the late nineteenth century the American China Development Company[15] was established to energize American capitalism abroad. China was regarded as "one of the most promising fields for American enterprise, industry, and capital."[16] The change and transformation had long been concepts of sentimental value in American culture. According to Mark Sullivan, the open-door policy "was set up in contrast to the 'spheres-of-influence' policy practiced by other nations...."[17] and thus Tang Tsou argues, "America was deeply inspired by the vision of a huge country with an ancient civilization transforming herself into a modern, democratic, Christian nation and following the lead of the United States."[18] This Open Door policy, however, failed because it was basically imperialistic and coercive.[19] The economic and market incentives behind the policy shrank, especially after the Qing empire collapsed from internal decay.[20]

The succeeding Nationalist government was embroiled in an atmosphere of confusion and disintegration. According to *The China White Paper*, U.S. foreign policy objectives were to maintain an "equality of commercial opportunity" and "the territorial and administrative integrity and political independence of China."[21] The momentum of the American market attitude toward China between World War I and World War II was ratified by a tariff treaty—signed by J. V. A. MacMurray, envoy extraordinary and minister plenipotentiary of the United States of America and T. V. Soong, minister of finance for the Nationalist government of the Republic of China.[22] The Treaty between the United States and China Regulating Tariff Relations was described as "an earnest desire to maintain the good relations which happily subsist between the two countries, and wishing to extend and consolidate the commercial intercourse between them."[23] Nevertheless, America's interests were quickly washed away by increasing Japanese military expansion and political malingering. Eventually, the end of the Nationalist government and the rise of the People's Republic of China (PRC) separated China's growth into a socialist state from the evolution of a global market economy.

America's second attempt at a foreign policy toward China failed during the Mao era (1949–1976).[24] Sino-American relations sank to their lowest level, especially in the late 1950s due to the loss of common ground on economic issues. After 1949, the PRC under Mao's ideology, repudiated any ideas related to a Western market economy. Market potential during the Mao period was close to zero because Mao's ideology prevented him from looking at Sino-American relations in terms of economic potential.

In addition, debate about the American economy was overwhelmingly clouded by calls for containment and the fear of the spread of communism (from the former Soviet Union to China and from North Korea to Indochina).[25] But the "containment policy"[26] was ineffective because American militarism was not a proper tool in which to modify China. According to one of the chief architects of the Containment Policy, Robert S. McNamara,[27] the escalation of military confrontation, armament struggle, and political maneuvering at the time of the cold war were nothing but the "misperceptions and mistrust that exist to this day."[28] In addition, military spending during the Cold war came to be regarded as unnecessary, if not a total waste.[29] The Vietnam War made no direct contribution to the economic well-being of the people in Southeast Asia. Moreover, according to Hans Morgenthau, the United States would also have to bear the moral obligation for the catastrophes and huge human losses incurred in Vietnam.[30]

After the death of Mao in 1976, Deng Xiaoping's leadership marked the first time that a market economy was implanted in mainland China's state policy. Sino-American relations were first secured on the basis of a mutual development toward fortifying the market economy. Nowadays, many scholars still argue over contemporary U.S.-China relations. Observing the approaching third phase of America's Chinese foreign policy—trade and economic cooperation—they arrive at two contrasting views. One side looks at Sino-American relations with caution and skepticism; the term "fragile relations" is used by Harry Harding to describe the fragmented and discretionary nature of U.S.-China relations since Nixon's visit in February 1972.[31] Other more sanguine scholars have used the term "Greater China" to predict the overwhelming economic development and political power of the collaboration of mainland China, Taiwan, and Hong Kong as a zone of influence.[32] Nevertheless, some of these scholars look at the potential of the Chinese economy and want to begin economic and business relations with China. The most notable advocate of the latter view is William Overholt, who strongly supports Chinese economic development and continued growth. Under such circumstances, the possibility of China's internationalization would be greater.[33] China's economic growth in 1995 was 9.8 percent,[34] and the huge potential market demands of a population of 1.23 billion[35]—are attractive to American investors.

Both views are part of the contemporary picture of Sino-American relations. However, many important ingredients of U.S.-China relations have not yet been addressed. In the first place, the advocates of the "China Threat" underestimate the force of the market economy that has already been modifying China into closer relation to the world economy rather than being locked into a pure, idealistic socialism. Moreover, the norms of the market economy and patterns of international organizations, underlying it are accepted by countries involved in global trading and market transactions. The engine has already started and will not be reversed without great economic and political costs. Furthermore, for those who have absolute confidence in the economic development of China and for those who only look at the Chinese economy alone should bear in mind that the international political economy has been an agent of modification in certain individual societies. With reference to these problems and questions, this book will look at the transformation of the market-oriented U.S. policy toward China.

The Layout

The vicissitudes of American foreign policy toward China, with particular emphasis on the motif of modernizing China through the construction of AML, will be detailed in the following chapters. Part one lays out the basic line of argument. Chapter 2 provides a framework for analysis. The logic of America's market liberalism will be detailed, as will the notion that AML engenders America's long-established foreign policy dating from after World War II. The theoretical debate of the causes of economic development in Japan and the Four Little Dragons, an indigenous or exogenous growth, is as current as ever. Apart from contrasting the general theories toward development and the feasibility of Confucianism in understanding Asian economic growth, other empirical literature dealing with Sino-American relations will be surveyed. My perspective of AML will be explored in order to understand the exogenous factor of the constitution of a market economy embedded within the auspices of U.S. foreign policy.

Part two details the early construction of U.S. market augmentation policy. Chapter 3 demonstrates the fundamental picture of the world political economy underpinned by American foreign policy initiative through the exogenous market force. To counterbalance the spread of communism from the former Soviet Union and the PRC, Japan was forced, economically as well as politically, into a corner, ensuring the fortification of capitalism. Chapter 4 details the establishment of the U.S. embankment of the market force in the Four Little Dragons, paving the way to become a second prong to contravene communism. These two flanks, during the cold war, served as tools of Communist China containment. After the opening of China in 1978 and the approach of the termination of the cold war, these two flanks facilitated engagement and served as models of demonstration to Communist China.

Part three analyzes the augmentation of U.S. policy toward China. Accordingly, chapter 5 will first analyze the cold war syndrome of foreign policy orientation by studying the strategic triangle. Then, it investigates the predicament of Communist China's isolation during its early development after the Communist Party took over the mainland in 1949. Mao's ideological containment drove him to isolate China from the global market economy. The outbreak of the Korean War reinforced U.S. containment policy. China collaborated with the Soviet Union to engulf the ideological as well as economic differences between the socialist camp and capitalist camp. The Great Leap Forward (1958–1960) and the Cultural Revolution (1966–1976) caused internal strife. As the 1960s and 1970s marked the height of economic development in Japan as well as in the Four Little Dragons, China's isolation revealed that a lack of market incentives created a profound adverse effect on its economic growth.

President Nixon of the United States laid the groundwork for China's rapprochement with the world economy after his visit in February 1972. In chapter 6, Nixon's visit will be analyzed in light of new findings, specifically a common interest in the wheat-trading opportunity. The development of Sino-America relations in this particular historical junc-ture was an externalization of market forces, as the gold standard col-lapsed at the same time. This chapter details why, how, and to what extent the incident affected Sino-American relations.

Chapter 7 examines the mutual coordination of China's economy with the world market economy. China's continued growth and devel-opment aroused world attention. In terms of China's coordination with the world economy, its application to the General Agreement on Tariffs and Trade (GATT), later the World Trade Organization (WTO), and the World Bank consolidated China's pace toward developing a market economy. The coordination of the trading opportunity between China and the world economy will be studied through its relations with the major trade regime, the GATT/WTO.

Part four focuses on post-cold war Sino-American policy trajectories. Chapter 8 illustrates the readjustment of China's economic development and its foreign relations with the United States after the cold war. The engagement and enlargement of U.S. policy toward China are said to constitute the new orientation of U.S. long-term strategy. Cooperation and conflict between these two countries are attracting major worldwide attention on, for example, the disputes between intellectual property rights, the Taiwan issue, and the most-favored-nation (MFN) status. The post-cold war global political economy sustains the AML of U.S. foreign rela-tions with China. The future prospects of foreign relations between them will therefore be revealed so as to probe a thread of inquiry for the orien-tation of foreign relations between them in the foreseeable future.

In conjunction with the approach of AML, chapter 9 discerns some possible theoretical implications that clearly accompany contemporary Sino-American relations in the arena of the international political economy. First, China's involvement in the world economy is all-en-compassing, as the interaction between China and the United States becomes intense. Second, U.S. policy toward China demonstrates a monitoring function on China's interdependence with the world economy. Finally, China's Third World role is being changed and trans-formed. Part five, chapter 10 will serve as the summary and conclusion to my overall research findings.

Sources and Data

Primary sources, specifically U.S. congressional hearings and trea-ties will be used fairly to track the development of U.S.-China foreign policy. The reasons behind using the hearings are: (1) accessibility; (2) hearings, whether being held on committee or subcommittee levels, are standard procedures to initiate a bill in the House or the Senate[36]; (3) hearings are good ways to look at not only the practitioners' view points but also the other opinions drawn from the society at large. More often than not, people from business groups, academic circles, and "careerists and ins-and-outers," including foreign policy elites, the executives of large firms, and academic professionals, are substantially influential in foreign policy-making.[37]Although congressional hearings cannot reveal everything about U.S. foreign policy, they indicate the discourse of the U.S. foreign policy. Like the political party, the hearing functions as the articulation of ideas and the aggregation of opinions.

Other resources, such as presidential memoirs, books, and journals either in English or Chinese are used regularly throughout this book. In terms of locating first-hand and source material for the American side, I was awarded a scholarship from the Eu Tong Sen Memorial Exchange Program, which enabled me to study as well as conduct research at the University of Hawaii in the fall of 1995. Hence, the Government Documents Section in the Hamilton Library at the University of Hawaii served as a valuable source of governmental archives.

Moreover, the University Services Center at the Chinese University of Hong Kong provided archival resources for locating historical newspapers in all Chinese provinces from 1949 to the present. The United States Information Service (USIS) in the Hong Kong American Consulate General also generously provided updated information about contemporary American politics under the categories of *Backgrounders* in economics, foreign policy, and politics.

Notes

1. Jeffrey E. Garten was the Under Secretary of Commerce for International Trade from 1993 to 1995. See Jeffrey E. Garten, "Business and Foreign Policy," *Foreign Affairs* 76, no. 3 (May/June 1997): 67–79.
2. In economics, there is a term called externalities. It refers to "the costs or benefits of a transaction that are incurred or received by members of the society but are not taken into account by the parties to the transaction." Richard G. Lipsey and Peter O. Steiner, *Economics*, 6th ed., (New York: Harper and Row Publishers, 1981): 424. The U.S. market-oriented policy toward China resembled a similar trajectory. In addition, I also analyzed the application of the concept of social cost to the U.S.-China relations in another occasion. See Gordon C. K. Cheung, "A Social Cost Approach to the Intellectual Property Rights Dispute between the United States and China" *Issues and Studies* 32, no. 12 (Dec. 1996): 111–123.

3. Karl Polanyi, *The Great Transformation* (Boston, MA: Beacon Press, 1944).
4. Ibid., 3.
5. Edward J. Nell, *Making Sense of a Change Economy: Technology, Markets and Morals* (London: Routledge, 1996): 51.
6. Alfred D. Chandler, Jr., *Scale and Scope: The Dynamics of Industrial Capitalism* (Cambridge, MA: The Belknap Press, Harvard University Press, 1990).
7. Hans Blommestein and Michael Marrese, *Transformation of Planned Economies: Property Rights Reform and Macroeconomic Stability* (Paris: OECD, 1991). Of course, there is more literature covering the privatization of former socialist states; this one serves as an example only.
8. Susan L. Shirk, *The Political Logic of Economic Reform in China* (Berkeley and Los Angeles: University of California Press, 1993): 334.
9. Margaret M. Pearson, *Joint Ventures in the People's Republic of China* (Princeton, NJ: Princeton University Press, 1991): 213.
10. G. John Ikenberry, "The Future of International Leadership" in *American Leadership, Ethnic Conflict, and the New World Politics*, edited by Demetrios James Caraley and Bonnie B. Hartman (New York: The Academy of Political Science, 1997): 18.
11. Rudyard Kipling, *If* (London: Phoenix, 1996): 17–19.
12. John D. Hicks, *A Short History of American Democracy* (Boston, MA: Houghton Mifflin Co., 1949): 322–323.
13. William Appleman Williams, *The Tragedy of American Diplomacy*, new edition (New York: W.W. Norton and Company, 1972): 45.
14. Ibid., 56.
15. Ibid., 40.
16. Ibid., 49.
17. The quotation is adopted in George Kennan's book. See George F. Kennan, *American Diplomacy 1900–1950* (New York: The New American Library, 1951): 24.
18. Tang Tsou, *America's Failure in China 1941–50* (Chicago: The University of Chicago Press, 1963): 5.
19. William Appleman Williams, *The Tragedy*, 120.
20. See Theda Skocpol, *State and Social Revolution: A Comparative Analysis of France, Russia, and China* (Cambridge University Press, 1979), 68–81 and Barrington Moore, Jr., *Social Origins of Dictatorship and Democracy: Lord and Peasant in the Making of the Modern World* (London: Penguin Books, 1969): 162–227.
21. *The China White Paper, August 1949* (Stanford, CA: Stanford University Press, 1967): 1.
22. Ibid., 12.
23. Ibid., 445.
24. Although President Richard Nixon paid a historic visit to China in February 1972, the formal agreement between China and the United States was only signed in 1979.
25. Thomas J. McCormick, 2d ed., *America's Half-Century: United States Foreign Policy in the Cold War and After* (Baltimore, MD: The Johns Hopkins University Press, 1995): 114–122.
26. The policy of containment was derived from a double source. It was derived from the 1947 Truman Doctrine, the 1948–1952 Marshall Plan, and the establishment of the North Atlantic Treaty Organization (NATO) in 1949. See ibid., 72–98.
27. Robert S. McNamara, *Out of the Cold: New Thinking for American Foreign and Defense Policy in the Twenty-first Century* (New York: Simon and Schuster, 1989).

28. Ibid., 100.
29. Ibid., 91.
30. Hans J. Morgenthau, *Politics Among Nations: The Struggle for Power and Peace* (brief ed. rev. Kenneth W. Thompson) (New York: McGraw-Hill, Inc., 1993): 248–9.
31. Harry Harding, *A Fragile Relationship: The United States and China since 1972* (Washington, DC: The Brookings Institution, 1992).
32. David Shambaugh, ed., *Greater China: The Next Superpower?* (Oxford: Oxford University Press, 1995) and Harry Harding, "The Emergence of Greater China: How U.S. Policy will have to Change" in *The American Enterprise* (May/June 1992): 47–55.
33. William H. Overholt, *The Rise of China: How Economic Reform is Creating a New Superpower* (New York: W.W. Norton and Company, 1993).
34. The Economist Publications, *The World in 1996*, 88.
35. Ibid.
36. Edward S. Greenberg and Benjamin I. Page, *The Struggle for Democracy*, 2d ed., (New York: HarperCollins, 1995): 412.
37. Thomas J. McCormick has detailed interrelations among these people in shaping and even formulating American foreign policy, either in the cold war or post-cold war era. See Thomas J. McCormick, *America's Half-Century: United States Foreign Policy in the Cold War and After*, 2d ed., (Baltimore, MD: The Johns Hopkins University Press, 1995): 7–16.

Part One

Theory

2

A Framework for Analysis

*The Chinese economy is already too complex to
be governed entirely by administrative
measures rather than by market forces.[1]*
—Harry Harding

Introduction

The AML of U.S. policy toward China emerged out of the U.S. perpetuation of developing a structured market economic force in the Asian-
Pacific region, a transformation policy characterized by change and
modification. The major theme of this chapter rests on the theoretical
investigation of how the exogenous variable of AML, facilitating first
as American foreign policy toward Japan and the Four Little Dragons,
will influence the ultimate transformation of China.

This chapter will be divided into three sections. The first section
will explore two alternative views which deal with the endogenous
explanation of Asian-Pacific growth. The second section will survey
other empirical studies of Sino-America relations. Finally, I offer my
perspectives on AML. AML offers an alternative way to study the exogenous effect of market-oriented U.S.-China policy.

Two Alternative Views:
Development Theories and Confucianism

In understanding Asian-Pacific economic development, there are two
widely used approaches: the development theory and theory of Confucianism. Developmental theories became popular in the 1950s and the
1960s as a way of explaining how postcolonial countries and territories
developed. The theory of Confucianism, however, was relatively new

in the 1970s and 1980s as an alternative to understand the so-called miracle of Asian economic growth. Outlining these two theories serves as a contrast to the perspective of AML that is used throughout this volume.

Development Theories

The search for a theory of development reached its climax in the 1960s when many former colonial states achieved their independence. There are many theories within this category; for the purpose of analysis, three of them will be explained. They are: W.W. Rostow's modernization theory, Andre Gunder Frank's theory of underdevelopment, and Mancur Olson's theory of distribution coalition.

The concept of development has long been a debated—not only in terms of its meaning, but also in the context of how development is achieved. In his book, *The Stages of Economic Growth*, W. W. Rostow postulated a theory which leads to a wide debate on the path, or the *right* path, toward economic development. His theory extrapolates a linear path of development. He posits that all societal development can be categorized into five stages: "the traditional society, the preconditions for take-off, the take-off, the drive to maturity, and the age of high mass-consumption."[2]

Rostow's theory provides a way of explaining economic development. However, his theory has not been free of criticism. Obviously, Rostow's theory strongly emphasizes the automatic process of the various stages. Once it starts, it proceeds as has been projected. The theory ignores the fact that once the engine of economic growth has started, many unforeseen and unexpected political and social problems might arise,[3] particularly when economic growth involves income redistribution of the economy at large. Second, Rostow's theory is an ideal-type which offers an *a piori* explanation for every country. He uses Russia, the United States, Great Britain, China, Sweden, and other countries to support his theory. But, if we want to substantiate this theory and apply it to Japan's economic growth and that of the Four Little Dragons, it would be less accurate. Economic growth in these countries depended upon their individual uniqueness in the formulation of government policies which can be characterized as an endogenous force. But, the major impetus comes from the exogenous U.S. market liberalism encapsulated in its foreign policy framework.

A. G. Frank's thesis is one among a few that falls within the world-system and dependency approaches. The main idea of Frank's theory is "the development of underdevelopment." In fact, economic development and underdevelopment are the opposite faces of the same coin—both generate economic development and structural underdevelopment. Throughout history, economic development in Latin America resulted from the legacy of the colonial powers' expropriation and appropriation. Structural underdevelopment came from the exploitative relationship between the metropolis and satellite states. Metropolis states referred to the colonial powers, such as Portugal and Spain in the seventeenth and eighteenth centuries. Now, they refer to developed countries such as the United States, Britain, France, and so forth. The satellite states are those developing countries which have long been exploited by colonial powers. The exceptions are Latin American countries, such as Brazil and Chile.

By using a historical approach, Frank concentrates his argument on the capital accumulation of the metropolis and the exchange relationship with the periphery. He uses three main stages in world capital accumulation and capitalist development: the mercantilist stage (1500–1700); the industrial capitalist stage (1770–1870); and the imperialist stage (1870–1930).[4] They illustrate how capital had been distributed unevenly throughout the historical process. Besides, the development process itself is biased and capitalist countries produce polarization by expropriation of economic surplus from developing countries.

Although Frank's theory paints a general picture of the nature of underdevelopment, we should ask why some countries, no mater how heavily dependent on foreign investment, are poor and others are rich. For example, Japan was nearly destroyed by a self-created war. However, its export-led strategy and postwar economic development enabled it to become the leading export country without being affected by the underdeveloped nature of growth. Canada was heavily dependent on foreign trade with Britain and France in the early nineteenth century.[5] Now, it is one of the members of the G-7 industrialized countries. Therefore, it would seem that to apply Frank's theory to other countries other than those in Latin America, it is still questionable and in need of further investigation.

In order to understand development among nations, one may suggest the ways of modernization (W.W. Rostow), or the ways in which a country can imitate or follow the footsteps of the developed countries in a similar pattern. Or, one might condemn the international environment, the exploitative world systematic structure (A. G. Frank) to the underdeveloped nature of many developing countries. However, in his book, *The Rise and Decline of Nations: Economic Growth, Stagflation, and Social Rigidities*, Mancur Olson attempts to use "distributional coalitions"[6] to explain why nations become stagnant (economically, socially, and politically). A possible way to prevent a country from declining is to search for a way that prevents "sclerosis"[7] from infecting the whole body of the country by those organizations such as, unions, institutions, and any established governmental or nongovernmental structure. It demands more liberal economic policies and pluralistic political measures.

Distribution coalitions refer to "the organizations for collective action within societies that we are considering are therefore overwhelmingly oriented to struggles over the distribution of income and wealth rather than to the production of additional output."[8] In other words, the tariff barriers inflicted on the importable, trade unions within a single country, and cross-industrial labor organizations are nothing but barricades to growth because they work in a way not to produce but to reinforce the robustness of those organizations. To use an analogy, the collective action or interest of those organizations resemble the cells in a human body. The collaboration and mingling with some kinds of cells in a human body might cause some long-term deficiencies to the whole. In so doing, the continuation and development of those organizations may eventually differentiate the aims between the organizations themselves and the nation as a whole. In the long-run, this is not healthy and may contribute to a nation's decline.

To summarize, the rational choice theory of group action indicates a culmination of individual interests that may contribute to the collapse of nations (although unnoticeable). The use of this theory in comparative politics rests on the fundamental understanding of the causes of increases and decreases of nations at large. When Rostow first gave his "non-communist manifesto" in 1960, it served as a fundamental guide for many developing countries by demonstrating the methods and different ways of growth. Olson's theory first appeared in 1965, and served as preventive theory. To prevent the decline of nations from accelerating, one has to pay attention to the rational expectation of individuals and the collaboration of groups—regardless of their level of economic development. A comparative finding of relations between development theories and the growth of Japan, the Four Little Dragons, and China is depicted as follows:

TABLE 2.1
The Inadequacy of Using Traditional Theories of Development to Explain the Economic Development of Japan, the Four Little Dragons, and China

Theories of Development	Characteristics	Degree of Applicability	Why?
W.W. Rostow: Stages of Economic Growth	Linear Development	Medium	Not all the states have gone through these stages
G.A. Frank: Development of Underdevelopment	Marxist Perspective	Weak	Simply cannot explain those countries' growth
Mancur Olson: Distributional Coalition	Rational calculation of group may hinder the countries' growth	Unknown	The economic development of the Four Little Dragons are still undergoing the process of growth

In conclusion, the complexity and subtleties of development studies rest on the identification of an appropriate perspective in the analysis of proper cases. According to the above comparison, the economic development of Japan, the Four Little Dragons, and China should be understood in a way that not only provides a casual understanding of the meaning of development (in an endogenous sense) but also enables us to distinguish the features that underpin the different developmental paths of those countries. Broadly speaking, both the structural theories of stages of growth and underdevelopment, and the rational group action theory, aim at indicating some factors which may lead to development or underdevelopment. The lack of these theories may impair the growth process among different countries. Nevertheless, examples of the development of the Four Little Dragons indicate that an understanding from the developmental angle is highly insufficient. Apart from the construction of a development theory, the search for a common experience among these countries deserves exploration. This exploration will therefore depict the workings of the market as the rudimentary force which engenders the long-established U.S. foreign policy objectives in the transformation and modification of Asian-Pacific economies. We will now turn to the Confucian way of understanding Asian economic growth patterns.

Confucianism

The economic development of postwar Japan and the fast growth of Asia's Newly Industrialized Economies (NIEs) arouses the curiosity as well as the suspicion of many social scientists: they search for explanations for these peculiar phenomena. Many of them, such as Peter Berger, Hsin-Huang Michael Hsiao and Siu-lun Wong have come up with a cultural explanation for these economic miracles. Their interpretation of the relationship between culture and economy reopened the question that Max Weber had asked in his book *The Protestant Ethic and the Spirit of Capitalism*.[9] In this book, Weber attempts to investigate the origin of the spirit of capitalism in relation to the "the magical and religious forces."[10] This idea is particularly related to Western Puritanism and modern capitalism. That said—since the use of culture as an explanation of economic development is in itself problematic—even Anthony Giddens, the author of the introduction to the English version of *The Protestant Ethic and the Spirit of Capitalism*, criticized that "Weber's statement of the connections between Puritanism and modern capitalism is based upon unsatisfactory empirical materials."[11] Nevertheless, the use of culture to understand economic development across countries is still tempting to contemporary scholars.[12] To relate culture and economic development to contemporary settings, many theorists attribute Japan and the Asian Newly Industrialized Countries (NICs) development to Confucianism.[13]

Like many other sociologists, Peter Berger is interested in the myth and cultural history of Asian countries. His personal encounters and interviews in various Asian countries such as South Korea, Taiwan, Japan, Singapore and Hong Kong propelled him to derive an "East Asian development model."[14] The assumption, or the major ingredient, of the Asian model maintained that "both Japan and the newly industrialized countries of East Asia belong to the broad area of influence of Sinitic civilization, and there can be no doubt that Confucianism has been a very powerful force in all of them."[15] The powerful force of Confucianism is interpreted by Hsin-Huang Michael Hsiao as the "Confucianist moral definition of the state."[16] The Confucian tradition of Asian countries, therefore, enables the state to freely mobilize humans as well as effectively use bureaucratic authority.[17] Michael Hsiao emphasizes the family and work organization as characteristics deeply embedded in Confucian thinking.[18]

In fact, the central issue of the Confucian familial idea is used extensively by Siu-lun Wong as a model to analyze the modernization of Hong Kong's economy.[19] Acknowledging the tradition of family ties and the subordination of paternalism, Wong suggests that the so-called "paternalistic management"[20] is the key to Hong Kong's successful economy. In particular, the "being-one's-own-boss" mentality of many Hong Kong people also gives rise to the vibrant and vigorous economic and industrial growth of Hong Kong.[21]

The above-mentioned represent some ways in which Confucianism is used to understand Asian economic growth. Many of these ideas extensively use Confucian doctrines such as family relations, respect, the hierarchical structure of kinship, the management of society, and so forth, as their center of argument. Nevertheless, it has to be pointed out that Confucianism is a very broad concept and does not only include the two founding fathers, Confucius and Mencius. As a concept, Confucianism, has a long and broad definition. Using the book of Confucius as an example, *The Analects of Confucius* contains conversations between Confucius and his students, fostering the way of governance and the crux of human relations.[22] For instance, in Book 16, Ji Shi, Confucius has substantiated his idea of equality by saying that "For when wealth is equally distributed, there will be no poverty; when the people are united, a small population will not matter much; and when there is stability throughout the land, there will be no such things as peril and subversion."[23] It is clear that his idea of government concerns the fairness of society. The connotation is closer to socialism than capitalism. Again, the sense of growth and economic development transcends less in the original spirit of Confucius.

Furthermore, if Confucianism has such profound and positive effects on economic development, why are North Korea, Thailand, and Burma still suffering from poverty. The Korean peninsula was a Chinese territory centuries ago and Thailand and Burma have substantial Chinese populations. Finally, to put it more bluntly, Ezra F. Vogel argued that "If Confucianism alone explains why countries modernize, why should the Confucian motherland lag behind? It is true that after 1949, failure can be attributed to socialist planning, but China had not achieved widespread industrialization before 1949, either."[24] As mentioned earlier in this section, the usefulness of Confucianism in the explanation of Asian development provokes many unanswered questions which are subject to further consideration. Moreover, this section has earlier suggested that many endogenous variables enable one to better understand Asian development. The purpose of mentioning two alternative views—development theories and Confucianism, is to provide a contrast to my postulation of the exogenous force of market liberalism.

Other Empirical Studies of Sino-American Relations

U.S.-China relations is a big topic. To understand their relations without the proper perspective will only result in either descriptive or speculative analyses. In addition, U.S.-China relations changed dramatically in the cold war and the post-cold war era. Therefore, I shall only examine some of the major literature published after 1990.

David Shambaugh introduced a new perspective in Sino-America relations. He puts forward in the introduction that he treated himself as a person who looked at Sino-U.S. relations from the Chinese perspective. In so doing, the bias would be reduced. His effort was highly appreciated especially his research ability in accessing the Chinese source. However, his "perspective" of using a Chinese angle is greatly challenged, particularly in terms of his opinions toward "China's America Watchers."[25]

Among the others, Harry Harding's *A Fragile Relationship* was a comprehensive account of Sino-America relations after 1972.[26] The contents of this book were useful as a reference tool in familiarizing myself about some important events which influenced Sino-America relations. Yet, as indicated by the title, it lacked the theoretical grasp that explains the logic behind their foreign relations. On the contrary, William Overholt was optimistic toward Chinese economic development and reform of China.[27] After reading his book, one might be persuaded to invest in China right away. However, on second thought, this rosy picture fails to present the development of China in a more analytical way. In addition, the fact that Overholt was managing director for a Hong Kong financial company reduced the book's impartiality.

Nicholas R. Lardy convinced readers of a robust Chinese economy by referring to important statistics and tables.[28] His expertise in understanding China from an economic angle earned him a due reputation. But, apparently, this book was one of the many products assigned by the funded-institutes. As soon as analysts and researchers were looking for a resourceful and analytical volume to guide them through the post-cold war era in Sino-America relations, Thomas W. Robinson and David Shambaugh edited a collection of current Sinologists' interpretations of U.S.-China relations.[29] It was indicative as well as theoretical, although the material was all useful, it was futile to draw a coherent line of thought among all the experts.

In 1995, two books related to U.S.-China relations were published by the National Textbook Company. Robert Rowland endeavored to illustrate U.S-China relations by describing some current issues such as human rights, trade, and military problems. But a central theme or theoretical framework was missing.[30] Lynn Goodnight et al. edited an enormous array of newspaper hightlights, speeches, magazines articles, and excerpts from different journals.[31] As the book's subtitle rightly mentioned, it was a "complete resource handbook." It served as a time-saving research. But it was only a tool.

Rosemary Footes's uncompromising argument distinguishes her from many sinologists.[32] Withholding a very strong argument of hard and soft power relations, she saw U.S.-China relations as one example of hegemonic U.S. influence, with a strong sense of cold war spirit. Nevertheless, as Samuel Kim put it, "She is somewhat less successful in describing and explaining the turns and twists of the Sino-American relationship in the post-normalization period, especially from 1989 to 1994."[33] My line of argument, however, is different from her in the light of coordination of market forces, not the conflictual nature of practicing of power. Compared with Harry Harding, Robert S. Ross saw U.S-China relations after 1972 as cooperation.[34] The mode of cooperation between China and the United States was based on their strategic relations. The theme that underlies his argument indicated that it was an imperative of the U.S. choice to cooperate with China in a strategic manner. Since their relations were strategical, it was situational, not on the genuine understanding with each other.

Quansheng Zhao used the micro- and macro-linkage approach to address China's foreign relations.[35] It seemed that his first two chapters appropriately handled the two concepts in theoretical terms. But, the empirical findings did not coherently match the theory. In addition, the linkage approach was previously used by Kuang-Sheng Liao in his understanding of the relations between antiforeignism and the modernization of China.[36]

A controversial, if not provocative, book called *China Can Say No* was written by some young Chinese reporters and intellectuals in 1996.[37] As the five authors mention, the book was not intended to be academic but instead provided an overview of Sino-American discourse relations. Although the book was praised by the *Beijing Review* as "well-reflected views shared by many others,"[38] the contents of the book were subjective and restricted.

Some scholars in the post-cold war era, nevertheless, still place Sino-American relations within a framework of military confrontation. For example, in a recent issue of *Foreign Affairs*, Richard Bernstein, Ross H. Munro, and Robert S. Ross debated the military expansion of China.[39]

Bernstein and Munro perceived China as an immediate threat while Ross saw China as potential threat. Their differences and disagreements appeared as a matter of degree, not substance.

The above-mentioned scholars either treat Sino-American relations as an area of disparate issues or still maintain and analyze Sino-American relations in light of a cold war understanding. The following perspective, nevertheless, hopes to bridge the theoretical and the empirical gap.

Alternative Perspective:
Market as an Exogenous Forces of Modification

The market, nevertheless, does not necessarily preclude the function of autonomous effects of individual states in generating prosperity and economic development. However, it would also be a grave mistake if the function of the market as a transformation agency could not be addressed from the developmental process of the facilitation of U.S. foreign policy. As Peter F. Drucker posits:

> The economy will, to be sure, remain a market economy—and a worldwide one.... the market, for all its imperfections, is still vastly superior to all other ways of organizing economic activity—something that the last forty years have aptly proven. What makes the market superior is precisely that it organizes economic activity around information.[40]

Culminating with foreign assistance, trade, FDI and the opportunity to access world markets, the shield of capitalism forces a self-generated sense of acceptance with market regulation among Japan, the Four Little Dragons, and China in particular. The enclosure of the socialist countries by the market economy of the United States during the cold war is clearly explained by James Fallows. He says that "...it is important to build a ring of states around China that are stable and independent. They would not be a military buffer against China, but they could be a political buffer."[41] However, the above statement represented the most common theme in cold war interpretation.

From the angle of market transformation, Alfred D. Chandler, a Harvard professor of business history, has demonstrated that a market that develops out of dynamic competition among industrial enterprises acts as a transformative agent in modifying individual societies. He added that

> these industries, in turn, were the pace setters of the industrial sector of their economies—the sector so critical to the growth and transformation of national economies into their modern, urban industrial form.[42]

In the cases of the growth patterns of Japan, the Four Little Dragons, and China in particular, the transformative effect of the global market on the individual economy is clearly engendered by U.S. political and economic influences after the World War II under the trajectory of an AML.[43] To analyze the perspective of AML, we have to look at the international structure, the regional structure, and the process.

International Structure

The argument of the perspective of AML begins from the U.S. establishment of an international political and economic environment which facilitated the development of the cold war as well as the construction of international economic institutions. U.S. policy toward China has always been engendered by a perpetual force of the International Political Economy (IPE) which was created under the auspices of U.S. initiatives. The market force echoed in the Asian-Pacific region allowed for an environment favorable to approaching China. Such an AML became clear especially when China began her economic reform by adopting market forces as a strategy for domestic growth and internationalization.

AML refers to the evolutionary process of U.S. foreign policy with respect to a structural change of the world political economy. Many components characterize that change. First, in terms of international politics, the United States engineered a comprehensive foreign policy initiative after World War II by implementing the Truman Doctrine in 1947, the Marshall Plan during 1948–1952, and the establishment of NATO in 1949. Moreover, its international economic relations were also characterized by the construction of many regimes endorsed by the U.S. Those regimes included the International Monetary Fund (IMF) in 1945, the General Agreement on Tariffs and Trade (GATT) in 1947 and the International Bank for Reconstruction and Development (IBRD) in 1945 (later called the World Bank).

No sooner had the United States constructed a world development model based upon market forces than was international politics dichotomized into two camps, the capitalist and the communist. Sharper and more distinguished counteracting forces between communism and capitalism thereafter emerged. On the one hand, states that were prosperous, stable, and economically developed belonged to the capitalist camp. On the other hand, revolutionary, unstable, and backward states were characterized as socialist. The function of U.S. foreign policy was the linchpin for regulating, stabilizing, and even "policing" the world from the thrust of socialism.

Many theorists such as Robert Gilpin, Robert Keohane, and Charles Kindleberger characterize the above-mentioned phenomena as the facilitation of America's "hegemonic stability." The unique leadership of the hegemon through the bestowing of punishment and the provision of reward gives rise to sustaining and enforcing stability in a region.[44] Although the theoretical development of hegemonic stability has a long tradition beginning with the rise of the Netherlands in the fifteenth and sixteenth centuries, the dominance of Great Britain in the eighteenth and nineteenth centuries, and the United States in the twentieth century, provide typical examples of changes in hegemonic power. Here we will explore the subordination of the market economy under U.S. foreign policy orientation.

Regional Structure

In the Asian-Pacific region, AML was facilitated by the creation of an ideal market economy which would strengthen American interests in the region and protect the region's stability from the threat of an encroaching communist ideology. The theoretical assumption behind AML is that the United States has been maneuvering its foreign policy machinery to build up a two-pronged foreign policy establishment which can fortify its interests in the Far East as well as have a modifying effect on China's future course of development. As noted in the *New York Times*, "In a sense, the flowering of trade with China is an extension of American intentions in Asia that dated from the 1950s and 1960s, when the United States opened its markets to exports from Taiwan, Singapore, and Hong Kong to help counter communism through growth."[45]

The encroachment[46] of Japanese economic and political settings led to the first prong of the market force. The embankment[47] of the economic development of the Four Little Dragons with U.S. influence served as the second prong of market encirclement. "By opening its domestic markets and by applying liberal economic principles without demanding reciprocity (at least not until recent times)," according to Michael Yahuda, "the United States has made it possible for first Japan and then the East Asian NIEs to follow policies of rapid economic growth that combined various mixes of export orientation and import substitution."[48] The containment policy of the United States and the disassociation of China from the world economy confirmed that U.S. foreign policy was unsatisfactory, especially during the 1960s and the 1970s.

As time went on, foreign policy between the United States and China changed as China changed with prevailing market forces. U.S. policy toward China, swung from containment to engagement.

By helping China to become economically developed and politically stabilized, the United States was constructing a consolidated base for its foreign policies towards China. Although their establishment clings to the cold war theory, both their modeling effects and functions of modifying China are not inevitable. Together with China's internationalization, the U.S. economic foreign policy toward China are as popular as ever. They have had the expected result, although it has been very slow.

The Process

The theoretical rationale that parallels U.S. foreign policy with market liberalism is important because of a self-perpetuating, self-correcting market liberalism. It "selects behaviors according to their consequences."[49] The countries which learn this concept can follow the creed of market forces, even though the guidance of American leadership is shrinking, especially in the post-cold war era. The pathological change of individual economies under America's influence is categorized as follows:

TABLE 2. 2
A Typology of the Developmental Process of U.S. AML toward China

	Japan	The Four Little Dragons	China
Foundation of Development	Structural Economic and Constitutional Change	Decolonization and Growth with international Market Demand	Socialism
Economic Structure	Market Capitalism	Small-Open Market Economy	Socialist Market Economy[1]
Growth Pattern	Trade	Trade	Trade[2]
Foreign Policy Objective	Encroachment	Embankment	Engagement
Prospects	Economic Superpower	Developed Economies	Market Economy

[1] The incorporation of the socialist market economy as the linchpin of national development strategy was adopted into the Constitution of the People's Republic of China at the First Session of the Eighth National People's Congress on 29 March 1993.

[2] The importance of trade to China is demonstrated by the pressing need of China to enter the WTO, an effort that has been put forth since 1986. See Harold K. Jacobson and Michel Oksenberg, *China's Participation in the IMF, the World Bank, and GATT: Toward a Global Economic Order* (Ann Arbor: The University of Michigan Press, 1990).

The above line of thought begins with understanding the foundation of development for Japan, the Four Little Dragons, and China. American foreign policy toward these three different types of countries has differed in terms of magnitude. Japan's economic and political structures were heavily transformed by a strategic and formal policy of U.S. encroachment right after World War II. The Japanese bellicose military environment was ameliorated by the introduction of a unique constitution during the Occupation period (1945–1952). By the same token, the economic system of Japan was transformed to an open and capitalist economy that served to strengthen America's interest in containing the spread of communism from the Soviet Union and China. Such transformation enabled Japan to be integrated and incorporated into the world market system.

In addition, the developmental path of the Four Little Dragons is similar in that they were former colonies. The end of colonization gave rise to the urgent search for a viable path of economic growth. Facing limited resources, most notably unreliable land use in the economy, they collectively adopted an export-led growth strategy.[50] These countries were influenced by U.S. foreign policy and nurtured under the embankment of U.S. capitalist market forces. The United States offered them market potential. The nurturing of these small economies reinforced America's interest in building up a ring of capitalist shields which were originally aimed at the counteracting force toward communism.

In contrast to the strategy that the Four Little Dragons had adopted, the PRC's strategy for development was replaced by the Communist government in 1949, China began to be transformed from a capitalist system to a communist system. Learning from the Soviet Union especially during the 1950s, China set itself apart from Japan and the Four Little Dragons. U.S. foreign policy during the cold war was characterized by a policy of containment.

Among others, a strategic triangle was one of the most powerful analytical tools in studying relations among the United States, China, and the former Soviet Union in the cold war. At that time, relations of the strategic triangle switched from a marriage between the Soviet Union and China in the 1950s, to the "rapprochement" of the United States with the Soviet Union in the 1960s. The game of changing partners continued in the 1970s and 1980s.[51] The demise of the Soviet Union, however, weakened the strategic triangle as an analytical tool. Furthermore, such a foreign- policy pattern enormously reduced the element of trust while increasing the costs in espionage and the possibility of conflict escalation.[52]

The Chinese economic system changed as time went on and as the ideological struggle in China ameliorated. The economic system during Mao's period (1949–76) was mainly socialist and the state's influence was profound. When China adopted economic reforms after 1978, the economic system gradually moved toward a market economy and relied on market incentives. In 1993, the government of the PRC formally adopted a socialist market economy as the linchpin of national development.

Post-cold war Sino-American relations witness, on the one hand, a collaboration on the theoretical change in power relations, and on the other, an opportunity to converge the United States' interests with China's internationalization process and economic development. In other words, U.S. policy toward China has long been established in a manner of modification. The existing antagonism between the United States and China is somewhat of a short-term setback. However, it will not affect the long-term trajectory of the modification motif of U.S. policy toward China.

International affairs have seen a greater emphasis placed on the use of "low politics." For example, economic foreign policy as a mode of cooperation and coordination in regulating foreign policy among nations. The prospect of AML and U.S. foreign policy toward China rely on the reinforcement of America's established power of coordination and the facilitation of the economic regimes such as the WTO in regulating the economic and political order in that region. China's alarming economic growth has moved her closer to a market economy and away from a pure socialist economy. Its role in the global economy, the continuation of its internationalization process and its Third World status are three implications underpinning China's relations with America's AML in the foreseeable future. Nevertheless, the split of mainland China and Taiwan would be an obstacle to Sino-American international cooperation. As Harry Harding argues:

> if Americans demanded evidence that China was moving toward capitalism and democracy, then much more economic and political liberalism would be necessary. Even some of the more modest American economic objectives required further transformation in China.[53]

The engendering of the AML not only facilitates American interests in the Asian-Pacific region but also circumscribes its foreign relations within a manageable regime of coordination and cooperation. The study of China's economic development and its relations with the United States coincides, therefore, with the search for political management of the relations between these two powers.

Notes

1. Harry Harding, *A Fragile Relationship: the United States and China Since 1972* (Washington, DC: The Brookings Institution, 1992): 308.
2. W. W. Rostow, *The Stages of Economic Growth: A Non-Communist Manifesto*, 3d ed. (Cambridge: Cambridge University Press, 1990): 4.
3. Malcolm Gillis et al., *Economics of Development*, 3d ed. (New York: W. W. Norton and Company, 1992): 26.
4. A. G. Frank, *Capitalism and Underdevelopment in Latin America* (London: Monthly Review Press, 1967). In the early part of this book, Frank tries to describe underdevelopment. Then, he follows by examining Latin America's economic structure, historical underdevelopment, and existing situation.
5. Bo Sodersten, *International Economics*, 2d ed. (London: Macmillan, 1980): 98.
6. Mancur Olson, *The Rise and Decline of Nations: Economic Growth, Stagflation, and Social Rigidities* (New Haven, CT: Yale University Press, 1982): 44.
7. Ibid., 217.
8. Ibid., 44.
9 Max Weber, *The Protestant Ethic and the Spirit of Capitalism*, trans. Talcott Parsons (New York: Charles Scribner's Sons, 1958).
10. Ibid., 27.
11. Ibid., 11.
12. Samuel P. Huntington, *The Clash of Civilizations and the Remaking of World Order* (New York: Simon and Schuster, 1996).
13. Peter L. Berger, "An East Asian Development Model?" in *In Search of an East Asian Development Model*, ed. Peter L. Berger and Hsin-Huang Michael Hsiao (New Brunswick, NJ: Transaction Publishers, 1988): 7.
14. Ibid., 4.
15. Ibid., 7.
16. Hsin-Huang Michael Hsiao, "An East Asian Development Model: Empirical Explorations" in *In Search of an East Asian Development Model*, ed. Peter L. Berger and Hsin-Huang Michael Hsiao (New Brunswick, NJ: Transaction Publishers, 1988): 18.
17. Ibid.
18. Ibid., 20.
19. Siu-lun Wong, "Modernization and Chinese Cultural Traditions in Hong Kong" in *Confucianism and Economic Development: An Oriental Alternative?* ed. Hung-chao Tai (Washington, DC: The Washington Institute Press, 1989): 166–186.
20. Ibid., 174.
21. Ibid., 176.
22. There are twenty books altogether in *The Analects of Confucius*. They are all dialogues, which distill many abstract ideas of governance into workable disciplines of day-to-day practical norms. See *The Analects of Confucius*, trans. Lao An (Shandong: Shandong Friendship Press, 1992).
23. Ibid., 281.

24. Ezra F. Vogel, *The Four Little Dragons: The Spread of Industrialization in East Asia* (Cambridge, MA: Harvard University Press, 1991): 84.
25. Ironically, his book was challenged from a Chinese perspective. See *China Book Review* (in Chinese), no. 2 (November 1994): 5–14.
26. Harry Harding, *A Fragile Relationship: The United States and China Since 1972* (Washington, DC: The Brookings Institution, 1992).
27. William H. Overholt, *The Rise of China: How Economic Reform is Creating a New Superpower* (New York: W. W. Norton and Company, 1993).
28. Nicholas R. Lardy, *China in the World Economy* (Washington, D.C.: Institute for International Economics, 1994).
29. Thomas W. Robinson and David Shambaugh, eds., *Chinese Foreign Policy: Theory and Practice* (Oxford: Clarendon Press, 1994).
30. Robert C. Rowland, *United States Policy toward the People's Republic of China: An Overview of the Issues* (Lincolnwood, IL: National Textbook Company, 1995).
31. Lynn Goodnight, James Hunter, and Eric Truett, eds., *Changing the Policy of the United States Government toward the People's Republic of China* (Lincolnwood, IL: National Textbook Company, 1995).
32. Rosemary Foot, *The Practice of Power: U.S. Relations with China Since 1949* (Oxford: Clarendon Press, 1995).
33. Samuel S. Kim, review of *The Practice of Power: U.S. Relations with China Since 1949*, by Rosemary Foot, *American Political Science Review* 91, no. 1 (March 1997): 231.
34. Robert S. Ross, *Negotiating Cooperation: The United States and China, 1969–1989* (Stanford, CA: Stanford University Press, 1995).
35. Quansheng Zhao, *Interpreting Chinese Foreign Policy: The Micro-Macro Linkage Approach* (Hong Kong: Oxford University Press, 1996).
36. Kuang-Sheng Liao, *Antiforeignism and Modernization in China*, revised and enlarged (Hong Kong: The Chinese University Press, 1990).
37. This book was also published by a Hong Kong Publisher. Qiang Song, et al., *China Can Say No* (Hong Kong: Ming Pao Publishing Ltd., 1996).
38. Cheng Si, "Chinese Say 'No' to the United States," *Beijing Review*, October 21–27, 1996, 13.
39. See Richard Bernstein and Ross H. Munro, "The Coming Conflict with America" *Foreign Affairs* 76, no. 2 (March/April 1997): 18–32 and Robert S. Ross, "Beijing as a Conservative Power" *Foreign Affairs* 76, no. 2 (March/April 1997): 33–44. Actually, Richard Bernstein and Ross H. Munro expand upon their ideas in a new book published in 1997. Richard Bernstein and Ross H. Munro, *The Coming Conflict with China* (New York: Alfred A. Knopf, 1997). See Also Andrew J. Nathan and Robert S. Ross, *The Great Wall and the Empty Fortress* (New York: W. W. Norton and Company, 1997).
40. Peter F. Drucker, *Post-Capitalist Society* (New York: HarperCollins Publishers, Inc., 1993): 181.
41. James Fallows, *Looking at the Sun: The Rise of the New East Asian Economic and Political System* (New York: Vintage Books, 1995): 352.
42. Alfred D. Chandler, Jr., *Scale and Scope: The Dynamic of Industrial Capitalism* (Cambridge, MA: Harvard University Press, 1990): 593.
43. Instead of being a specific concept, AML refers to the conventional phenomenon that can be traced back to American foreign policy that affected the world economy at large and the Asian-Pacific economy in particular. In a recent article entitled "Paradigm Lost," Richard N. Haass put forth the idea of augmented realism as the principle of American foreign policy in the post-cold war era. See *Foreign Affairs* 74, no. 1, 43–58. Nevertheless, the term "realism" may coincide

with the Cold War's atmosphere of military confrontation. An AML approach will, on the contrary, have a greater implication in the light of enlargement of opportunity to the nation that enjoys being a participant of the world market economy.

44. Robert Gilpin, *The Political Economy of International Relations* (Princeton, NJ: Princeton University Press, 1987): 72–80. See also Charles P. Kindleberger, *Power and Money: The Economics of International Politics and the Politics of International Economics* (New York: Basic Books, 1970) and Robert O. Keohane, *After Hegemony: Cooperation and Discord in the World Political Economy* (Princeton, NJ: Princeton University Press, 1984).
45. Seith Faison, "China Export Boom Also Benefits U.S." *International Herald Tribune*, 5 March 1997, 1.
46. Literally, encroachment refers to the gradual military, economic and political changes that Japan was forced to change during the early 1950s onward, especially during the Occupation.
47. Embankment is defined as "the act or process of embank". See Webster's New World Dictionary, 3d College Edition (New York: Prentice-Hall, 1994): 442. The embankment or fortification of capitalist market forces closely resembled the economic development of the Four Little Dragons.
48. Michael Yahuda, *The International Politics of the Asia-Pacific, 1945–1995* (London: Routledge, 1996): 12.
49. Kenneth N. Waltz, "Political Structures" in *Neorealism and Its Critics*, ed. Robert O. Keohane (New York: Columbia University Press, 1986): 84.
50. Although many of them adopted the import substitution policy, the policy of export promotion enabled them to begin the path of economic development and the cooperation with the world economy.
51. Lowell Dittmer, "The Strategic Triangle: A Critical Review" in *The Strategic Triangle: China, the United States and the Soviet Union*, Ilpyong J. Kim, ed., (New York: Paragon House, 1987): 36–40.
52. Min Chen, *The Strategic Triangle and Regional Conflicts: Lessons from the Indochina Wars* (Boulder, CO: Lynne Rienner Publishers, 1992).
53. Harry Harding, *A Fragile Relationship: The United States and China Since 1972* (Washington, DC: The Brookings Institution, 1992): 215–216.

Part Two

U.S. Construction of the Asian-Pacific Market Economy

3

U.S. Encroachment of Japan

Together, our nations [Japan and the U.S.] have a
unique opportunity to help people the world over
to learn, to change the way they work, indeed, to
transform how they live. We must seize this
opportunity because it is also our responsibility.[1]
—U.S. President Bill Clinton

Introduction

This chapter will examine the overall foreign policy orientation of the United States toward shaping Japan, as the first prong of a capitalist market economy, to accommodate U.S. long-term modification of Japan—eradication of the communist threat by peaceful economic means. We will see how the market fortification of Japan was engineered under U.S. foreign policy. By referring to congressional hearings and formal treaties signed between the United States and Japan, the encroachment of Japan under AML will be highly distinguished.

Japan as a Cornerstone of Market Liberalism

To understand the change in U.S. orientation from containment to economic pacification, one should first examine different countries that had various relations with the United States. This line of thought stems from the restructuring of Japan from a militarily defeated country to one of the world economic powers. It is also my first argument. This restructuring was a cornerstone for U.S. consolidation of Asian political stability as well as a strengthened counteraction of swiftly expanding communism. The Occupation period from 1945 to 1952 laid the foundation for a new constitution and a democratic model for Japan to abide by.

The postwar international atmosphere gave rise to a unique U.S. influence. According to John W. Dower, the Asian-Pacific region at the time was like a lake to the United States. One of the ways to protect that lake from communist infringement was "to build Japan into an anti-communist workshop and base."[2] Nevertheless, the Occupation period was clouded by the military containment policy that circumvented the Pacific and was implemented with U.S. naval and military might. Naval bases were situated around the Pacific Ocean, from Hawaii to the Ryukyus, from Guam-Saipan to the Philippines, as a way to counteract the spread of communism.[3] Developed as a model for the achievement of capitalism, Japan was still regarded "as a military base against China and the Soviet Union, but also as an industrial base supporting the counterrevolutionary cause in Southeast Asia,"[4] particularly during the Occupation. Japan benefited from U.S. foreign policy in the Korean War (1950–53). According to Chalmers Johnson, "the Korean War was in many ways the equivalent for Japan of the Marshall Plan."[5] Many war necessities such as clothing were supplied by Japan because of its geographical location and its role as a capitalist cornerstone against communism.

Japan's internationalization process, its position in the international economy in general and in GATT in particular, was subject to conflicting opinions. Almost all the member countries rejected Japan's full membership in GATT, except the United States, West Germany, Canada, Italy, and the Scandinavian countries.[6] For example, Britain opposed Japan's joining for fear that it would not abide by the rules governing member states.[7] According to Komiya and Itoh, "no country besides Japan has ever been discriminated against in the GATT system, whether legally or illegally."[8] Against all odds, in 1955 Japan, bolstered by the United States, joined GATT as a full member. In return, Japan had to voluntarily restrain[9] its exports to the United States. Its foreign policy afterwards was inevitably allied with that of the United States. It also reinforced its function as a capitalist shield against communist threats from the Northwest.

Japan was greatly strengthened by its incorporation into GATT, the largest world trade organization. Its products penetrated the world market freely, if not relentlessly, from garments and cotton-wear in the 1960s to automobiles in the 1970s, from computers in the 1980s to super chips and biochemical products in the 1990s.[10] Again, as shown by the enormous support of the United States during the Korean War, Japan's industrial growth was at the top of its own developmental agenda as well as one of the major concerns of the United States in securing the Asian-Pacific economy and stability.

The huge U.S. balance of payment (BOP) deficit in trade with Japan is a clue to understanding the underlying motive of the United States— a trade-off between Asian-Pacific stability with capitalist consolidation and the pain of a huge BOP deficit. Starting from the "Textile Wrangle" dispute over Japanese cotton in the U.S. market in 1953, Japanese and U.S. trade has always been a contentious topic in their foreign relations. The height of this dispute was over autos and semiconductors. In August 1980, an estimated 250,000 U.S. workers were unemployed due to a flood of Japanese imports.[11] On 2 September 1986, Japan and the United States redundantly signed the U.S.-Japan Semiconductor Agreement. Japan made three commitments: "(1) to halt U.S. and third-market semiconductor dumping; (2) to provide increasing market access for foreign semiconductor companies in the Japanese market; and (3) not to undercut the Agreement in Japan."[12] Nevertheless, the Agreement did not function properly in reducing Japanese imports to the United States, which has become a long-lasting dilemma for the United States.

Weighing the immediate economic benefits versus long-term political stability in East Asia, the United States government still remained tolerant of the trade imbalance. During the Senate hearings of the Subcommittees on Asian and Pacific Affairs in 1987, Don Bonker, a member of the Committee on Foreign Affairs, testified that the leeway given by the United States to Japan and other Asian-Pacific countries had far-reaching consequences for maintaining stability in the region. He testified:

> Let me just conclude with one other question about USTR's [U.S. Trade Representatives] role with respect to unfair trade practices. Our discussion has been mostly on Japan. That is the subject of this hearing. But we have other countries in the Pacific rim who engage in similar policies, Korea and Taiwan, notably. And interestingly these three countries have been vital to U.S. political and security interests in the Pacific, and we wanted to see these countries strong economically so they could become strong democratically and help us keep the whole Pacific secure.[13]

The American market functioning as a liberalization agent, argued Bonker, still "provided Japanese industry an ample market for a wide range of products."[14]

Economic interdependence and security alliance are the two major loci of U.S.-Japan relations after the cold war. Although occurring very slowly, post-cold war economic relations between Japan and the United

States showed improvement. The long and unresolved question of the trade deficit remains the most important economic issue between these two largest trading nations in the world. In May 1989, under section 301, Japan was cited by the Bush administration for unfair trading of supercomputers and satellites.[15] However, the nature of section 301 has allowed it to stick onto America's individual trade sanction with little welcome by international organizations such as GATT or the WTO. U. S. and Japanese trade negotiations still consist of continuous bilateral talks and conferences. The Japan-U.S. Structural Impediments Initiative (SII) talks ended in June 1990. Japan agreed to spend 430 trillion yen for public works over a ten-year period. It also completed a thorough review of the then-existing land taxation reform, hoping to liberate the Japanese investment atmosphere by initiating more favorable terms for foreign investors.[16]

A transformation of U.S. "get-tough" economic coercion policies to "get-smart" engagement policies was based on talks begun in the 1990s.[17] As suggested by Paula Stern, former chairwoman of the U. S. International Trade Commission, "the United States and Japan should work toward creation of an international code of investment to limit governmental interference in companies' international operations and a code on competition to harmonize antitrust policy."[18] In that sense, future U.S.-Japan talks should rely more on an institutional framework and existing codes of conduct rather than a mercantilist focus on tariffs or sanctions. The 1993 Framework Talk between the U.S. and Japan facilitated negotiation and cooperation in a formal and regular manner.

The full name of The Framework Talk was "A Joint Declaration on the Framework for a New Economic Partnership between Japan and the United States." This all-encompassing declaration acted as an agenda that encourages both countries to identify areas in which cooperation or mutual exchange of ideas can take place. Apart from trade and commodities, many up-and-coming problems are also ready to be resolved. by the efforts of these two countries. Instead of mitigating the importance of trade issues, the Framework highlights Japanese involvement in world affairs; of course, under the auspices of the United States. The declaration postulates a "common philosophy" underlying the Japan-U.S. alliance: "that a combination of developments—shifting economic relations in East Asia, pressure inside Japan for that country to play a hegemonic role in the area, and the end of the Soviet military threat—could create a significant change in the relations between the United States and Japan."[19] Nevertheless, the visionary Framework Talks can

FIGURE 3.1
An Outline of Japan–U.S. Framework Talks

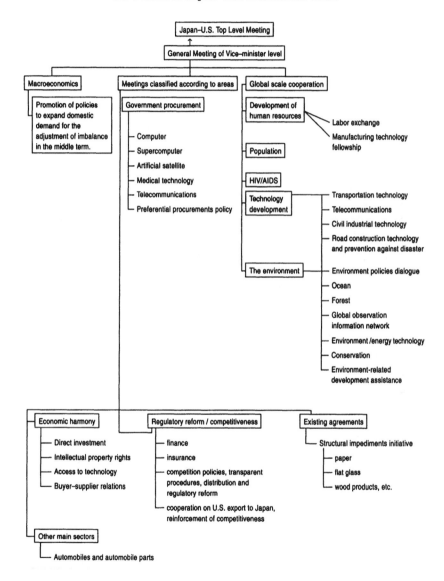

Source: *White Paper on International Trade Japan 1994* (Singapore: McGraw-Hill with the collaboration with the Ministry of International Trade & Industry (MITI), 1995), 127.

do little in reducing the immediate, huge trade deficit of the United States. The bilateral trade negotiations in February 1994 between President Bill Clinton of the United States and Prime Minister Masahiro Hosokawa of Japan ended in vain. Japan rejected America's demands for the opening of autos and auto parts, insurance, medical equipment, and telecommunications markets on the bases that the "quantifiable measures of progress on the opening of those markets" will inevitably "permit the United States to establish import targets for its products in Japan."[20] The collapse of the talks caused U.S. trade deficits with Japan to jump to a record high of $66 billion in 1994, 60 percent of which was due to imports of auto parts or cars.[21]

The plight of the trade deficit remained the same in early 1995. In April of that year, the U.S. trade deficit with Japan escalated to $5,874 million.[22] Resorting to traditional carrots and sticks, the United States threatened the Japanese government with an ultimatum of $5.9 billion worth of punitive tariffs on luxury Japanese cars made by Honda, Toyota, Nissan, Mazda, and Mitsubishi as most of them are made solely in Japan.[23] Their economic brinkmanship ended after Japan agreed to purchase $9 billion additional auto parts from the United States.[24]

If trade liberalization and an open market are two major objectives of the United States, the successful lesson in the auto industries will spill over to other sectors such as the insurance and fruit industries. More negotiations on the opening of the Japanese insurance market were carried out in July 1996 between U.S. Trade Representative Charlene Barshefsky and her counterpart from Japan, Trade Minister Shunpei Tsukahara. It is not yet clear whether the use of tariff threats worked in this circumstance. Regardless, the trade antagonism between the United States and Japan does not damage their security alliance. The security alliance and foreign relations between Japan and the United States are benefited by the gesture of the Japan relaxing its market.

While the U.S. government acts as Dr. Jekyll and Mr. Hyde in its economic relations with Japan (allowing substantial trade deficits each year while threatening Japan with tariffs to open its market), its security and military relations with Japan are more like Jack and Jill. If the end of the cold war is said to be the watershed of their military relationship, their relations are now *de facto* experiencing little alteration. The following table lists selected defense treaties between the United States and Japan.

Right after the demise of the former Soviet Union, many people questioned the presence of the U.S. troops in the Asian-Pacific and the Japa-

TABLE 3. 1
Treaties of Defense Signed by the United States and Japan (1985–1988)
(selected)

Date	Agreements	Concerns
5 July 1985	Assistance	Japan contributes 145,865,000 yen of military expenditure to the U.S. Forces (1985–1986)
17 June 1986	Assistance	Japan contributes 150,990,000 yen of military expenditure of the U.S. Forces (1986–1987)
10 September 1985	Acquisition and Production of P-3C Aircraft	Japan acquires 30 P-3C weapon systems and related equipment and materials
21 January 1986	Assistance	Training of Japanese self-defense forces
20 January 1987	XSH-60J Weapon System	The development of weapon systems by Japan
23 August 1988	Financial Contribution	Japan contributes 153,979,000 yen of military expenditure to the U.S. Forces (1988–1989)

1 The Mutual Defense Assistance Agreement between Japan and the United States of America was first signed in Tokyo on 8 March 1954.

Source: Department of State, "Defense Assistance: Agreement Between the United States of America and Japan," 5 July 1985, *Treaties and Other International Acts Series* (TIAS) 12000, no. 2957, 5; Department of State, "Defense: Acquisition and Production of P-3C Aircraft: Agreement between the United States of America and Japan," 10 September 1985, TIAS 12017, no. 3585, 2–3; Department of State, "Defense: Agreement between the United States of America and Japan," 21 January 1986, TIAS 12005, no. 2957, 2–3; Department of State, "Defense Assistance: Agreement between the United States of America and Japan," 17 July 1986, TIAS 12009, no. 2957, 5; Department of State, "Defense: XSH-60J Weapon System: Agreement between the United States of America and Japan," 20 January 1987, TIAS 12014, no. 2957, 2–3 and Department of State, "Defense, Financial Contribution: Agreement between the United States of America and Japan," 23 August 1988, TIAS 12028, no. 2957, 5.

nese-American Security Treaty, as the common threat from the Soviet Union vanished. However, the renewal of their Mutual Security Treaty on 23 June 1990 consolidated their alliance.[25] In a nutshell, Japan's security relations with the United States after the cold war transformed from comprehensive security under the protective umbrella of the United States to mutual cooperation with America in handling Asian and even international security issues, keeping the peace and protecting Asia's stability.

In terms of security and military cooperation, the U.S.-Japan security issue played a more important role than that during the cold war.

Because of the fall of the Soviet Union, the unique hegemonic role of the United States in the Asian-Pacific region has decreased. The United States has to find more justification for maintaining large numbers of troops in Japan. The potential threat of North Korea, the expansion of China (mainly economical) and the volatile Southeast Asian economy and political environment, have been deemed enough reason to maintain security ties with Japan. According to Song Young-sun, director of Japan Studies in Korea, the significance of the U.S.–Japan alliance lies in the joint research and development (R&D) projects in defense industries (e.g., Fighter Support Experimental [FSX]), continuation of America's East Asian Policy and the reaction of Japan's neighbors to Japan.[26]

U.S.-Japan cooperation in military R&D and the stationing of U.S. troops in Japan are *de facto* the most salient form of cooperation. According to Hisashi Nakamura and Malcom Dando, military R&D allows Japan and the United States to co-develop defense equipment and research military technology.[27] The mutual benefit reveals the exact nature of their post-cold war relations. On the one hand, Japan is obligated to the leadership and hegemonic role of the United States. On the other hand, the United States depends on technological transfers from Japan. As Peter J. Katzenstein and Nobuo Okawara contend:

> The increase in Japan's defense capabilities and the creation of a national option, brought about by linking Japan's national security to that of the United States, will undoubtedly have an effect on how Japan, its Asian neighbors, and the United States will react politically in an era of profound international and domestic change.[28]

U.S. troops stationed in Japan shows how close the link is between the United States and Japan. America has over 44,800 troops in Japan (mainly in Okinawa): compared to 36,250 in South Korea; 7,050 in Guam; 43,800 in Hawaii; 140 in Singapore; and 370 in Australia.[29] A crisis struck when a twelve-year-old Japanese girl was raped by three U.S. Marines in Okinawa in 1995. Some Japanese started questioning the maintenance of large numbers of U.S. troops in Japan, with Japan paying all expenses.[30] To restore the confidence of the Japanese and uphold U.S. interests in the Asian-Pacific region, President Clinton managed to sign a Joint Security Declaration with Prime Minister Hashimoto of Japan on 17 April 1996 and even called it "the cornerstone of stability throughout Asia."[31] A Joint Action Plan was also announced to cope with the problems U.S. troops caused in Okinawa, which included noise-reduction and a decrease in training and exercises in Okinawa.[32] This Joint Declaration called for mutual security cooperation[33] and reinforced U.S. interests in the Asian-

Pacific region. At the same time, it provided more latitude for Japan in reshaping its political role.

To move the focus from Japan to the Asian NIEs, we can discern more clearly how AML facilitates the long established influence of U.S. foreign policy. For China in particular, the objective of the United States is more explicit. According to Warren Christopher, former secretary of state of the United States, "Our policy will seek to facilitate a peaceful evolution of China from communism to democracy."[34] Before turning to China in the next chapter I will examine the implantation of an established market fortress of the Four Little Dragons, which played a role in the opening of the Chinese economy.

Notes

1. The statement was made during President Bill Clinton's address to the Diet in Japan on 18 April 1996. See USIS, "Transcript: President Clinton's Address to the Diet in Japan," *Foreign Policy Backgrounder* (19 April 1996): 7.
2. John W. Dower, "Occupied Japan and the American Lake, 1945-1950" in *America's Asia: Dissenting Essays on Asian-American Relations*, edited by Edward Friedman and Mark Selden (New York: Vintage Books, 1971): 148.
3. The thirty-three naval bases at twenty-two different locations in the Pacific were:
   1 Main Naval Base: Hawaii
   1 Major Operating Base: Guam-Saipan
   1 Major Operating Base, Caretaker Status: Manus
   2 Secondary Operating and Repair Bases: Adak, Philippines
   6 Secondary Bases, Small: Kodiak, Dutch Harbor, Attu, Midway, Samoa, Ryukyus
   7 Air Bases: Johnston Island, Palmyra, Canton Island, Majuro, Wake, Marcus, Iwo Jima
   4 Combined Air Bases and Fleet Anchorages: Kwajalein, Eniwetok, Truk, Palau
   11 Air Fields: Hawaii, Kodiak, Dutch Harbor, Adak, Attu, Midway, Samoa, Manus, Guam-Saipan, Philippines, Ryukyus
   Adapted from ibid., 161.
4. Ibid., 182.
5. Chalmers Johnson, *Conspiracy at Matsukawa* (Berkeley and Los Angeles: University of California Press, 1973): 23.
6. See Ryutaro Komiya and Motoshige Itoh, "Japan's International Trade and Trade Policy, 1955–1984" in Takashi Inoguchi and Daniel I. Okimoto, eds., *The Political Economy of Japan: vol. 2, The Changing International Context* (Stanford, CA: Stanford University Press, 1988): 178.
7. W.G. Beasley, *The Rise of Modern Japan* (London: Weidenfeld and Nicolson, 1990): 248.
8. Komiya and Itoh, "Japan's International Trade," 178.
9. It was called "voluntary export restrictions" (VERs). See ibid., 179–180.
10. Among others, the automobile and computer (including chips) industries became bones of contention between the United States and Japan in the course of trade negotiation. For the Japanese automobile industry's development, please

refer to Michael A. Cusumano, *The Japanese Automobile Industry: Technology and Management at Nissan and Toyota* (Cambridge, MA: Harvard University Press, 1985). For more information about the fights between the United States and Japan concerning the computer and semiconductor industries, refer to Clyde V. Prestowitz, Jr., *Trading Places: How We Are Giving Our Future to Japan and How to Reclaim It* (New York: Basic Books, Inc., 1988): chapters 9 and 10.

11. R. Komiya, M. Okuno and K. Suzumura, eds., *Industrial Policy of Japan* (London: Academic Press, Inc., 1988): 318.
12. House Committee on Foreign Affairs, *Developments in United States-Japan Economic Relations, May 1987: Hearings before the Subcommittees on Asian and Pacific Affairs*, 100th Cong., 1st sess., 23 April and 5 May 1987, 84.
13. Ibid., 148.
14. Ibid., 5.
15. Mike M. Mochizuki, "Japan and the Strategic Quadrangle" in Michael Mandelbaum ed., *The Strategic Quadrangle: Russia, China, Japan, and the United States in East Asia* (New York: Council on Foreign Relations Press, 1995): 126.
16. *Japan Economic Almanac 1991* (Tokyo: The Nikkei Weekly, Nihon Keizai Shimbun Inc., 1991): 9.
17. Paula Stern "U.S.-Japan Trade: Get Smart, Not Just Tough" Asia Pacific Issues, no. 12 (East-West Center, April 1994): 1–8.
18. Ibid., 4.
19. Martin Feldstein, "National Security Aspects of United States-Japan Economic Relations in the Pacific Asian Region" in Jeffrey A. Prongel and Miles Kahler, eds., *Regionalism and Rivalry: Japan and the United States in Pacific Asia* (Chicago, IL: The University of Chicago Press, 1993): 454.
20. *Time*, 21 February 1994, 15.
21. *International Herald Tribune*, 17 May 1995, 1.
22. United States Information Service "U. S. Trade Deficit Hits Record as Imports Rise, Exports Drop" in *News Release* (22 June 1995), 1.
23. *International Herald Tribune*, 17 May 1995, 1.
24. *International Herald Tribune*, 29 June 1995, 1.
25. Roger Bowen, "Japan's Foreign Policy" *Political Science and Politics* 25, no. 1 (March 1992): 57.
26. Yong-sun Song, "Prospect For U. S. Japan Security Cooperation" *Asian Survey* 35, no. 12 (December 1995): 1089–1091.
27. Hisashi Nakamura and Malcolm Dando, "Japan's Military Research and Development: A High Technology Deterrent" *The Pacific Review* 6, no. 2 (1993): 86–187.
28. Peter J. Katzenstein and Nobuo Okawara, "Japanese Security Issues" in Craig Garby and Mary Brown Bullock, eds., *Japan: A New Kind of Superpower?* (Washington, DC: The Woodrow Wilson Center Press, 1994): 1–72.
29. *Japan Economic Almanac 1996* (Tokyo: The Nikkei Weekly, Nihon Keizai Shimbun, Inc., 1995): 33.
30. Michael Blaker, "Japan in 1995: A Year of Natural and Other Disasters" *Asian Survey* 35, no. 1 (January 1996): 48.
31. United States Information Service "U. S.-Japan Partnership Cornerstone of Asian Stability" in *Foreign Policy Backgrounder* (19 April 1996): 1.
32. Ibid., 5.
33. *EIU Country Forecast, Japan, 2d Quarter* (London: The Economist Intelligent Unit Limited, 1996): 9.
34. William H. Overholt, *The Rise of China: How Economic Reform is Creating a New Superpower* (New York: W. W. Norton and Company, 1993): 365

4

U.S. Embankment of the Four Little Dragons

*A belief in progress and economic liberty would
have taken Asia part of the way to prosperity, but
it was free trade which gave Asia its big break.
Access to North American and West European
markets helped East and South-East Asian
economies to grow on the back of their exports.*[1]

—Chris Patten

Introduction

This chapter attempts to study how and to what extent U.S. foreign policy played the role of embanking a chain of capitalist market economies in East and Southeast Asia. The Four Little Dragons: Hong Kong, Taiwan, South Korea, and Singapore, were especially affected by such embankment. This was partly because all of them are small, open economies susceptible to outside influence, particularly concerning trade and export. Lucian W. Pye describes the four as having a "close involvement with the United States, both in terms of direct U.S. interventions—as during the occupation of Japan, the Korean War and Korea's subsequent recovery, and the years of substantial economic and military aid to Taiwan—and in terms of their continuing dependence upon access to the U.S. market."[2] Nevertheless, if one turns to the subject of international relations with the United States in foreign policy orientation, one discerns a dramatic and more subtle picture of their genuine cause of development—the pull of the U.S. market and deliberate encouragement.

Furthermore, the extent of America's foreign policy has been affecting the growth of the Four Little Dragons in the provision of a market impetus to serve as their guiding post. In the Final Reports of the Tenth American Assembly prepared by the American Assembly, the importance of U.S. assistance to the Far East is used as a foreign policy tool. The Report warned that:

> It is highly important that the Republic of Korea and Taiwan should increasingly demonstrate the success of cooperation with the free world. An important element in producing this result will be the steady development of a sense of hope and confidence in themselves and in their future which comes from economic progress and the tangible evidence that their efforts in this direction bear fruit.[3]

Given their economic growth, the result is a stark contrast between communist inefficiency and capitalist prosperity. I will discuss each of the Four Dragons below.

Hong Kong

Hong Kong's success, as argued by many analysts, is mainly due to its practice of *laissez-faire* or later, the government's positive non-intervention in industrial development and the construction of macroeconomic policies.[4] Moreover, the 1960s to the 1990s also saw the policies of transforming Hong Kong from an entrepôt of trade to a manufacturer in light industries, and from the base of labor-intensive knitting and garment production to the production of capital-intensive electronics. Furthermore, some people also attribute the economic development of Hong Kong to factors such as the overall structure of Hong Kong's economy, the financial system, the vigorous trade sectors and the legal system.[5]

At a glance, the aforementioned explanations are necessary conditions for Hong Kong's development, but not sufficient. Hong Kong's small and open economy is susceptible to the influences of the world market. In order to see this, Hong Kong's relations with the United States need to be explained.

Access to the United States market enormously affected the growth of Hong Kong's political economy. America has tremendous interests in Hong Kong, economic and political. The United States has more than 900 firms in Hong Kong. Furthermore, Hong Kong houses more than 200: more incredibly, 70 percent of these are headquarters of U.S. firms that conduct business in Asia. The American Chamber of Commerce in Hong Kong is the largest of the American Chambers in the world. Most U.S. firms that do business with China enter the mainland via Hong Kong. Of the $9 billion worth of U.S. exports to China in 1993, more than 36 percent passed through Hong Kong.[6]

As a colony of the British Empire for more than 150 years, Hong Kong's decolonization process will be very different from other former colonial states such as Malaysia, Singapore, Indonesia, and Vietnam.[7] The transformation of sovereignty from Britain to the PRC took place on 1 July 1997 as set by the Joint Declaration in 1984. To facilitate the monitoring of Hong Kong's evolution, the United States promulgated the United States-Hong Kong Policy Act in 1992. This Act allows the United States to monitor Hong Kong's political development after the hand-over. The United States is interested in the stability of Hong Kong including: (1) a smooth transition from British to Chinese sovereignty; (2) the protection of human rights in Hong Kong; (3) the democratization process; and (4) the strengthening of relations between Hong Kong and the United States.[8]

The history of U.S. interests in Hong Kong can be traced back to the 1850s when about twenty missionaries and merchants gathered together in Hong Kong.[9] The relation between Hong Kong's economic growth and the facilitation of America foreign policy did not take place until the World War II.

A dramatic change in the political economy of Hong Kong was initiated by the decision between U.S. and Hong Kong governments regarding illegal immigrants from mainland China during the early 1960s. It was clearly documented in a 1962 hearing of the congressional Subcommittee to Investigate Problems Connected with Refugees and Escapees[10] that the development of Hong Kong's economy was not arbitrary. Rather, it was orchestrated by the Hong Kong government with the consensus of the United States. Tackling the immediate problems of a large influx of refugees required the wholehearted support of the United States to open its market. The policy proved to be very effective. The refugee problems eased and Hong Kong's economy developed. The keynote speech made during the congressional hearing noted the fundamental change:

> The first way in which the outside world can help this colony with its burdens is to assure for the limited range of goods we can produce efficiently....These people's welfare depends upon our trade and, if our trade can be maintained with adequate scope for growth and without artificial restrictions, there is every chance that we can complete a task we first set ourselves twelve years ago. But the stifling of our exports would, sooner rather than later, transform this dynamic community into an international pauper and would thus create conditions in which massive and wholesale relief would be the only remedy.[11]

Moreover, according to Senator Kenneth B. Keating, who testified at the hearing, since "... this exodus can become a major political and psychological victory for the West in the conflict with communism,"[12] the logical action of the U.S. government is to use Hong Kong as a habitat for the refugees, demonstrating the prosperity of capitalism.

Hong Kong trade statistics indicate that exports to the United States increased, particularly after the 1962 hearing and the opening of the U.S. market.

As seen in table 4.1, the increase of Hong Kong exports to the United States was steady, averaging 8 percent per year between 1960 to 1970. The decrease in subsequent years was due to the climax of the Vietnam War and the expansion of other economies such as Japan and the former West Germany.

The increase in trade and the expansion of Hong Kong's export market propelled the economic development of Hong Kong and stabilized

TABLE 4.1
Area Distribution of Hong Kong's External Trade (in percentages)

Countries	1960	1965	1970	1975	1980
			Import		
United States	12.3	11.1	13.2	11.8	11.8
United Kingdom	11.3	10.7	8.6	5.1	4.9
China	20.2	25.9	16.1	20.3	19.7
Japan	16.1	17.3	23.8	20.9	23
Other	40.1	35	38.3	41.9	40.6
Singapore		2.7	2	5.7	6.6
Taiwan		1.7	4.7	5.8	7.1
All Countries	100	100	100	100	100
			Export		
United States	26	34.2	42	32.1	33.1
United Kingdom	20.4	17.1	12	12.2	10
West Germany	3.7	7.4	8	12.5	10.8
Japan	3.5	2.6	4	4.2	3.4
Canada	2.7	2.7	3.2	3.4	2.6
Australia	3	2.7	2.9	4.5	2.9
Singapore		2.8	2.3	2.7	2.6
Other Countries	40.7	30.5	25.6	28.4	34.6
All Countries	100	100	100	100	100
N. America and Europe	57.1	69.4	74.2	71.9	69.8

Source: Census and Statistics Department, *Hong Kong Trade Statistics*, various issues.

the then-unsteady relation then between the citizens and the government. This harmonization between society and government was later elaborated upon by Hsin-Huang Michael Hsiao. He commented: "Without favorable world economic conditions and U.S. support, East Asian states probably could not have enjoyed such autonomy and strength in state-society relationships."[13] The opening of the U.S. domestic market to Hong Kong exports raises the question of whether an imperialistic penetration and capitalist exploitation theory still holds. This question cannot be answered by A. G. Frank solely, as addressed in chapter 2.[14] Neo-Marxist Immanuel Wallerstein contended that "the *middle* (italics in original) stratum [semi-periphery] is both exploited and exploiter."[15] In that sense, it can be argued that the opening of Hong Kong's export market is a subtle form of capitalist expansion. The economic development of Hong Kong revealed the political function of U.S. foreign policy—facilitating a capitalist prong to stop the spread of communism. Moreover, the result is a non-zero-sum return in which both countries/places can benefit from a merging with the world market economy. A more detailed discussion of the gain from trade is provided by Bill Warren.[16] He argued that a more subtle and precise calculation of gains from trade is necessary if we want to know how developing countries can actually benefit from trading with developed countries.[17] His argument challenged greatly the Marxist view on the exploitation nature of the developed countries over the developing countries through trade and exchange.

In addition to economic benefits, the opening of the U.S. market to Hong Kong's exports also encouraged Hong Kong to participate in the world economy. Hong Kong participates in many international organizations, some of which are indicated in the following chart.

According to Richard W. Mueller, consul general of the United States in Hong Kong, "U.S. interests in Hong Kong are extensive and have grown along with the territory's prosperity and role in the international community. These interests will be maintained as sovereignty over Hong Kong shifts from Hong Kong's dynamism continue."[18] To maintain Hong Kong's international competitiveness, Mueller maintained that "The United States has been encouraged by the Joint Liaison Group's (JLG) action in extending 170 multilateral treaties currently applying to Hong Kong through the United Kingdom."[19] What is the dynamism of Hong Kong? It is the facilitation of the world market economy in moving some developing countries from poverty to prosperity. The former governor of Hong Kong, Chris Patten, also maintained that "The new eco-

TABLE 4.2
Hong Kong's Participation in International Organizations (selected)

Asian Development Bank

Asian and Pacific Development Center

Asian-Pacific Economic Forum

General Agreement on Tariffs and Trade (GATT)/World Trade Organization (WTO)

International Bank for Reconstruction and Development (World Bank)

International Monetary Fund

International Labor Organization

International Telecommunication Union

United Nations Commission on Narcotic Drugs

United Nations Conference on Trade and Development

World Health Organization

World Intellectual Property

Source: United States Information Service, "A Report to Congress on Conditions in Hong Kong as of 31 March 1993 as Required by Section 301 of the United States-Hong Kong Policy Act of 1992" in *Foreign Policy Backgrounder* (6 April 1993): 13–14.

nomic era worked because the United States economy took off after the war [World War II] and pulled the rest of the free-trade, free-market world with it. Access to the markets of North America and Western Europe made possible the growth of Asian economies."[20] In *The Economist*, Patten later concluded that there were two basic factors that gave rise to Asian development: a belief in progress and the pursuit of market-oriented policies.[21]

The experience of Hong Kong demonstrates that there is a link between its prosperity and economic take-off. The following section will be devoted to the study of South Korea to see how these factors contributed to its growth.

South Korea

The end of the Korean War (1950–53) not only split the country into two, but also fortified U.S. influence and the quadrangle of relations in northeast Asia with the Soviet Union and China.[22] It also bolstered South Korea's capitalist nature. In his original research on the course of Korea's capitalism, Carter J. Eckert maintained that "after Liberation, and especially after the Korean War, the United States was willing to some extent to assume the role of capitalist (elder brother) in Korea...."[23]

With the big brother giving military and economic assistance, the development of the Korean economy was not a random phenomenon but a salient case of U.S. AML, which resembled the situation in Japan. South Korea's formal relations with the United States began with their Mutual Defense Treaty signed on 1 October 1953 (implemented on 17 November 1954) by John Foster Dulles and Y. T. Pyun. But there was a difference in attitude between the two cases. Japan was regarded as an aggressor that needed to be restrained, while South Korea was considered a potential victim susceptible to "external armed attack"[24]

As seen from Article III of the Mutual Defense Treaty, the gist of U.S. and South Korean interests is clear:

> Each Party recognizes that an armed attack in the Pacific area on either of the Parties in territories now under their respective administrative control, or hereafter recognized by one of the Parties as lawfully brought under the administrative control of the other, would be dangerous to its own peace and safety and declares that it would act to meet the common danger in accordance with its constitutional processes.[25]

The 1950s and the 1960s were characterized by military confrontation between the communist bloc led by the Soviet Union and China and the capitalist bloc led by the United States and Japan. To strengthen the capitalist bloc, the United States gave more than $4 billion in economic and military aid to South Korea between 1953 to 1961.[26] The Military Assistance Program (MAP) provided troops, aircraft such as the C-45, and training.[27] Economic aid consisted of program loans and technical assistance.[28] During the height of the cold war (1965–69), U.S. defense expenditures increased tremendously. In 1965, the United States spent $83 million on defense; in 1967, $126 million; and in 1969, $342 million.[29] The expenditure was mainly to pay South Korean combat troops in Vietnam.[30]

The economic well-being and development of South Korea was considered during a congressional hearing by William J. Porter, former U. S. Ambassador in South Korea, to be a relatively slight preference as the economic environment for "normal competitive export" toward Korea's exports during a congressional hearing.[31] Although the chairman of these hearings, J. W. Fulbright might have regarded this circumstance as "incidental," markets from the United States and Japan to some in Southeast Asia and South America, opened to South Korean exports and were inevitably under the auspices of the United States.[32] As can be seen in table 4.2, the United States occupied the lion's share of South Korea's exports during the 1970s and the 1980s.

TABLE 4.3
Merchandise Exports by Principal Countries (1976–1985)

	1976	1977	1978	1979	1980	1981	1982	1983	1984	1985
					U.S.$1 million					
United States	2,493	3,119	4,058	4,374	4,607	5,661	6,243	8,245	10,479	10,754
Japan	1,802	2,148	2,627	3,353	3,039	3,503	3,388	3,404	4,602	4,543
Hong Kong	325	342	385	531	823	1,155	904	818	1,281	1,566
Indonesia	49	69	103	195	366	370	383	252	254	196
United Kingdom	254	304	393	542	573	705	1,103	1,005	956	913
Germany	398	480	663	845	875	804	758	775	924	979
Others	2,394	3,585	4,482	5,216	7,222	9,056	9,074	9,946	10,749	11,332
Total	7,715	10,047	12,711	15,056	17,505	21,254	21,853	24,445	29,245	30,283

Source: Korea: Managing the Industrial Transition, vol. 1, The Conduct of Industrial Policy (Washington, DC: The World Bank, 1987): 158.

Hagen Koo and Eun Mee Kim, Syngman Rhee in the 1950s, and Park Chung Hee in the 1960s, used the concept of South Korea as a bridgehead against communism as a bargaining chip for South Korea's development.[33] Although Park Chung Hee took office by military coup on 16 May 1961, his reorganization of the major capitalists (known as *chaebol*) and their alliances with the government on industrialization projects rejuvenated South Korea's economy. Koo and Kim contended that "it was this narrow development alliance between the military regime and select large capitalists that eventually shaped the capital accumulation process during the period of export-oriented industrialization."[34] South Korea's economic growth is generally characterized by a large-scale conglomeration of such industrial powers and reliance on market forces. Alice H. Amsden, in her book *Asia's Next Giant*, mentioned that "in the presence of large concentrations of market power, reliance on the market mechanism for reform appears to produce some perverse results, not just in Latin America but also in the Far East."[35] Relying on the market, South Korea's average gross national product (GNP) growth from 1962 to 1984 remained at 8.2 percent per year.[36] The post-cold war development of *chaebol* has seen expansion into East European countries. Samsung took the first initiative to set foot in Hungary: investment in color television factories.[37] Other *chaebols* followed suit; for example, the LG Group (formerly the Lucky-Gold Star) invested $410 million in Moscow and Daewoo Motor committed $1.1 billion to modernize Poland's car production.[38]

In December 1996, South Korea became the twenty-ninth member of the Organization for Economic Cooperation and Development (OECD), a recognition of its remarkable economic growth and development.[39] No sooner had South Korea joined than a new labor law was launched that allowed entrepreneurs to dismiss workers easily in an attempt to stop the downturn in Korea's economic competitiveness.[40] This abrupt change in labor policy resulted in an outcry from unions and a nationwide strike. In other words, South Korea has been self-generated to compete in the international market economy. The future continued growth of Korea depends on the international economy. The next section attempts to investigate the relations between Taiwan and the United States using the logic of AML.

Taiwan

The political, economic, and strategic position of Taiwan was not only included in U.S. long-term interest in the Far East but also became an irreconcilable antagonistic issue with mainland China. The United States perceives Taiwan as its tangible asset because "Taiwan clearly is capable of fulfilling its role by providing expeditious support to deter aggression and promote economic development throughout the region."[41] The fulfillment of Taiwan's role as the fortress against the spread of communism nevertheless provokes a sensitive nerve for China (the issue of sovereignty and integrity. Taiwan has long been regarded as the "renegade province" of the Mainland. According to Deng Xiaoping's comment on 26 June 1982, the formal position of the Mainland on Taiwanese issues is that there cannot be "complete self-determination"; however, the internal and municipal policy will be entirely up to Taiwanese jurisdiction.[42] It, therefore, demonstrates how important an issue Taiwan has become in Sino-America relations.

The historical relationship between Taiwan and the United States exhibits consolidated cooperation in many arenas. Militarily, the Seventh Fleet launched by Truman in 1950 demonstrated the wholehearted support of the United States in combatting an attempted communist invasion by mainland China.[43] Also, this movement activated the hostile feelings between the United States and the PRC, particularly in the late 1950s.[44] The twists and turns of U.S.-Taiwan relations arrived when the PRC and the United States normalized their relations through Nixon's February 1972 visit to China. The visit resulted in the Shanghai Communiqué signed on 27 February 1972. U.S.-Taiwan relations were "denormalized." By 1979, U.S.-PRC diplomatic relations were formalized. The U.S. embassy in Taiwan was "demoted" and became the American Institute. However, it still operated as a venue for unofficial U.S.-Taiwan relations. In addition, U.S.-Taiwan ties were never severed because the Taiwan Relations Act went into effect on 1 January 1979.

The Taiwan Relations Act, according to Harry Harding, was a significant act that even "from the Chinese perspective, simply perpetuated the American commitment to the island's security in a slightly different form."[45] Boldly argued by Ray Cline, senior associate of the Georgetown Center for Strategic and International Studies, before the Subcommittee on Separation of Powers on Taiwan issue, the Taiwan Relations Act only reflected the political reality between China and Taiwan.[46] He testified:

> The truth, as any idiot can tell you, by looking at the map and history of the forty years, is that in terms of present-day political organization, there are plainly two Chinas, two organizations of people, with authorities to pass their laws, duly con-

stituted, in two quite different political systems, in *de facto* control of their separate territories and people. Both claim to be, by right, the government of one China, or both Chinas, if you like, but actually, *de facto*, neither has been able to translate this claim into control of the population to territory of the other, since the People's Republic of China seized military control of the mainland in 1949.[47]

The Taiwan Relations Act, thereafter, became an instrument through which the United States could manipulate its China politics. By the same token, the "magic" Act bolstered Taiwan's security and, inevitably, fostered her pace for democratization at home and internationalization abroad. These acts serve as a gauge to test their foreign relations. And, just recently, this gauge indicates that closer relations between Taiwan and the United States have been reached. Together with other reasons, *this* is a reason to strengthen U.S.-Taiwan relations.

Second, according to Michel Oksenberg, the U.S. government would not allow "any unilateral action by Washington, Beijing or Taipei to alter this framework—such as through threats or use of force, excessive arms purchases or seeking change in formal status—would jeopardize American objectives."[48] The basic American objectives are the core element in maintaining a peaceful Asian-Pacific region and the unobstructed economic growth between mainland China and Taiwan.

Finally, the democratization and political openness of Taiwan nowadays provide it with stronger bargaining powers to lure the support of the U.S. Congress and their approval of military intervention if military confrontation between Taiwan and mainland China were to happen.[49] Theoretically speaking, the United States and Taiwan share a belief in the importance of democracy. When outside force is perceived as a threat to this common ideological ground, the U.S. government may react appropriately because "Once ideas become embedded in rules and norms—that is once they become institutionalized—they constrain public policy."[50]

Looking at this issue from an economic point of view, Taiwan relied heavily on American's aid in the 1950s and 1960s. Thomas Gold uses Taiwan's economic development as a case study to demonstrate that the so-called Taiwanese miracle is derived from the complex incorporation of government policy, colonial legacies from Japan (1895–1945), the development aid from the United States, and the interplay between the society and the state.[51] He contends that "Taiwan's specific situation of dependency yielded development, not underdevelopment" because "the social dislocations commonly associated with dependency, such as an impoverished rural sector and glaring inequality, have been

TABLE 4.4
The U. S. Trade Balance (May 1994) (in U.S.$1 million)

Countries	Bilateral Balance	Export	Imports
Hong Kong	233	935	703
South Korea	-299	1,347	1,645
Singapore	-118	1,150	1,268
Taiwan	-932	1,268	2,200
Total	-1,117	4,699	5,815

Source: USIS, *News Release*, 21 July 1994, 3.

largely eliminated."[52] Clearly, the limitation of the dependency approach in the light of Taiwan's development is astonishing, particularly since it has a small and open economy that is, theoretically, susceptible to fluctuations in the world economy, especially those in the United States. The above table shows the huge trade deficit that the United States has with the Asian NIEs.

Obviously, the trade deficit shown on the above table indicates that Taiwan relies greatly on U.S. support. Although it is understandable that bilateral trade may reflect the political implication of their mutual relationship, many believe that Clinton's Asian economic policy is more realistic and significant. With Japan's transformation from military autocracy to economic democracy after 1945, the translation of economic power to authentic democratic election in Taiwan enables the spread of capitalism and market forces. If U.S. national interest is also defined as the preservation of capitalism, the underwriting of Taiwan's race toward international recognition is inevitable. We now turn to the example of the last dragon, a new graduate of the process of economic development.

Singapore

Singapore experienced another unique experience of transformation from small, open economy into a universally recognized cosmopolitan city-state. U.S. foreign policy objectives in transforming Southeast Asia were initiated in 1959.[53] The facilitation of U.S. policy toward Asia in general and Southeast Asia in particular was confirmed in a study by the Committee on Foreign Relations. As suggested, U.S. foreign policy should aim at cooperation with some Asian countries because "...the growth of greater regional cooperation between the noncommunist states of Asia could do much to strengthen these countries and to forward U.S. policy objectives."[54]

Among other countries, Singapore's decolonization process strongly suggested its position in opposition to a communist threat[55] and the major role of the market force in its developmental process.[56] From 1945 to 1965, Singapore gradually and successfully consolidated the ruling party's (People's Action Party [PAP]) control. The end of World War II brought political chaos to Singapore. On the one hand, the British were hoping to sustain their influence and control. On the other hand, a "vacuum" in political control created increasing challenges from various aspects. In the late 1940s, the Singapore Progressive Party (SPP) and the Singapore Labor Party (SLP) were the major political forces.[57] According to Yeo Kim Wah and Albert Lau, the tutelage of British rule and collaboration with those parties collectively acted against the communist challenge because "through Emergency laws and the close patrolling of the Johore Straits, the government prevented communists from using Singapore as a base to provide supplies of food and arms to their comrades fighting the British in Johore."[58] The amelioration of the communist penetration into Singapore's soil signaled the country to formulate a strong and consolidated political force.

In 1954, the PAP was formulated by Lee Kuan Yew and other elites such as Lim Chin Siong and Fong Swee Suan. Eventually, PAP took power in 1959. As the ruling party drew its support from labor unions and Chinese schools and workers.[59] Until the independence of Singapore in 1965, struggles with both communism and ethnic problems were Singapore's major concern. Joining the Malaysia Federation with Sabah and Sarawak in 1963 was a testing ground for Singapore's endurance of racial discrimination. It proved to be failure because Lee demanded "Malaysian Malaysia,"[60] a fundamental contradiction with the ethnic and ideological principal of the Malay. Irreconcilability with this political idea eventually led Singapore to become an independent country on 9 August 1965.

Singapore's independence came during the height of the U.S. foreign policy of containment toward Communist China and the former Soviet Union. Since 1954, the Southeast Asian Treaty Organization (SEATO) not only serves as an "umbrella"[61] for the protection of Southeast Asia from communist infiltration but also served as venue for U.S. military involvement in that region. U.S. material and military support were colossal. More than 4.2 million soldiers and 120 billion U.S. dollars were rendered through SEATO in the war zone of Vietnam.[62] SEATO ceased to be a tool of U.S. military containment after the end of 1973.[63]

Although Singapore was not a member of SEATO, its participation in the Association of Southeast Asian Nations (ASEAN) on 8 August 1967, nevertheless, enlightened its economic role within cooperation among ASEAN members. After being expelled from the Malaysian Federation in 1965, Singapore actually facilitated its independent industrial and economic policy. Export-led growth strategy was later initiated in Singapore. It was called the "Second Industrial Revolution" (SIR) in 1979.[64] Among the other countries, the United States was the largest investor in the 1970s. In 1970, U.S. investment in the manufacturing sector, in terms of gross fixed assets, was 343 million, 34 percent of total investment in Singapore. In 1976, the number tripled to 1,233 million—32 percent of total investment in Singapore.[65] In addition, the mode of cooperation in ASEAN through economic integration gave rise to Singapore's reliance on the international market for its production and exports. In the 1980s the United States and the European Community (EC) comprised 40 percent of Singapore's exports.[66] Even in the early 1990s, U.S. investment still outperformed Japan and European investment. In 1992, for example, the U.S. invested $1,200.1 million; Japan, 843.4 million; and Europe, 613.9 million.[67]

After the cold war, Singapore changed its development strategy and implemented more government incentives. For example, the Singapore Trade Development Board (STDB) shaped and reformulated the overall promotion of Singapore's international trade.[68] According to the Economic Survey of Singapore conducted by the Singapore Ministry of Trade and Industry, Singapore's economy expanded by 10.1 percent in 1994. The main factor was the "recoveries in the key export markets and strong growth in the regional economies."[69] However, it has to be remembered that, the long-established developmental path of Singapore's growth has been toward the international political economy of which the U.S. influence was still a significant variable.

Summary

By using the Four Little Dragons as an example, I have illustrated U.S. AML. First, as argued in chapter 2, the influence of American foreign policy serves as an exogenous variable in light of understanding the economic growth of the Four Little Dragons. Second, the political implications of the economic success of the Four Little Dragons suggested to Communist China that market forces are a way out. Finally, the cases of the Four Little Dragons indicated that the international economy played a role in the process of local economic development. Nevertheless, the 1960s and the 1970s witnessed Chinese economic deviation from the path of the world developmental process. The following chapter will examine the predicament of China's isolation during the 1960s and 1970s.

Notes

1. *The Economist*, 4 January 1997, 21.
2. Lucian W. Pye, "The New Asian Capitalism: A Political Portrait" in Peter L. Berger and Hsin-Huang Michael Hsiao, eds., *In Search of an East Asian Development Model* (New Brunswick, NJ: Transaction Publishers, 1988): 82.
3. American Assembly, *Some American Views on U.S. Far Eastern Policy, 1956-57* (New York: American Institute of Pacific Relations Inc., 1958): 3.
4. H. C. Y. Ho, "Views on Hong Kong's Past Growth and Future Prospects" in *The Economic System of Hong Kong*, ed. H. C. Y. Ho and L. C. Lau (Hong Kong: Asian Research Service, 1992): 1–5.
5. David G. Lethbridge, ed., *The Business Environment in Hong Kong*, 2nd ed. (Hong Kong: Oxford University Press, 1984).
6. Hong Kong Government, *Hong Kong: America's Business Partner in Asia* (March 1994): 1.
7. Malaysia (then Malaya) was granted independence by the British empire in 1957. Singapore gained partial independence in 1957. After the struggle of the People's Action Party (PAP) established in 1959, Singapore acquired independence in 1965 after expulsion from the Malaysian Federation. Indonesia became independent in 1949. The formal independence of Vietnam was granted by the Geneva Agreement in 1954, an immediate result of the defeat of French troops in the same year.
8. United States Information Service, "A Report to Congress on Conditions in Hong Kong as of 31 March 1993 As Required by Sec. 301 of the United States-Hong Kong Policy Act of 1992" *Foreign Policy Backgrounder* (6 April 1993): 4.
9. Richard W. Mueller, "America's Long-Term Interest in Hong Kong" *U.S. Department of State Dispatch* 6, no. 21 (22 May 1995): 438.
10. Senate Committee on the Judiciary, *Refugee Problem in Hong Kong and Macao: Hearings Before the Subcommittee to Investigate Problems Connected with Refugees and Escapees*, 87th Cong., 2d sess., May 29; June 7, 8, 28; and July 10. U.S. Government Printing Office: Washington, DC, 1962.
11. Ibid., 166.
12. Ibid., 4.
13. Hsin-Huang Michael Hsiao, "An East Asian Development Model: Empirical Explorations," in Peter L. Berger and Hsin-Huang Michael Hsiao eds., *In Search of An East Asian Development Model* (New Brunswick, NJ: Transaction Publishers, 1988): 18.
14. In terms of Hong Kong's economic development, we have to look in detail at the relationship between it and the United States, since Frank's theory of underdevelopment can only provide a mechanical description of two separate identi-

ties. See A.G. Frank, *Latin America: Underdevelopment or Revolution* (New York: Monthly Review Press, 1970).

15. Immanuel Wallerstein, "The Rise and Future Demise of the World Capitalist System: Concepts for Comparative Analysis" *Comparative Studies in Society and History* 16 (1974): 405.
16. Bill Warren, *Imperialism: Pioneer of Capitalism* (London: Verso, 1980): ch. 8.
17. Ibid., 207.
18. Richard W. Mueller, "America's Long-Term Interests in Hong Kong" *in The ANNALS of The American Academy of Political and Social Science*, ed., Max J. Skidmore 547 (September 1996): 144.
19. Richard W. Mueller, "America's Long-term Interest in Hong Kong" *U.S. Department of State Dispatch* 6, no. 21 (22 May 1995): 439.
20. Cris Patten, "The Secret of Asia's Success" *South China Morning Post*, 12 April 1996, 21.
21. Cris Patten, "Beyond the Myths" *The Economist*, 4 January 1997, 20.
22. Robert G. Sutter, *East Asia and the Pacific: Challenges for U.S. Policy* (Boulder, CO: Westview Press, 1992): 93. See also Michael Mandelbaum, ed., *The Strategic Quadrangle: Russia, China, Japan, and the United States in East Asia* (New York: Council on Foreign Relations Press, 1995) for the post-Cold War perspectives on the Northeast Asia relations.
23. Carter J. Eckert, *Offspring of Empire: the Koch'ang Kims and the Colonial Origins of Korean Capitalism, 1876-1945* (Seattle, WA: University of Washington Press, 1991): 257.
24. Senate Committee on Foreign Relations, *United States Security Agreement and Commitments Abroad: Republic of Korea: Hearings before the Subcommittee on United States Security Agreement and Commitments Abroad*, 91st Cong., 2d sess., 24, 25, and 26 February 1970, 1717.
25. Ibid.
26. Hagen Koo and Eun Mee Kim, "The Developmental State and Capital Accumulation in South Korea" in *States and Development in the Asian Pacific Rim*, ed. Richard P. Appelbaum and Jeffrey Henderson (Newbury Park, CA: Sage Publications, 1992): 123.
27. Senate Committee, *United States Security Agreements*, 1550.
28. Ibid.
29. Ibid., 1743.
30. Ibid., 1541.
31. Ibid., 1584.
32. Ibid., 1585.
33. Hagen Koo and Eun Mee Kim, *The Developmental State*, 144.
34. Ibid., 125.
35. Alice H. Amsden, *Asia's Next Giant: South Korea and Late Industrialization* (New York: Oxford University Press, 1989): 137.
36. Ibid., 56.
37. Sharon Reier, "The Chaebol Gamble on East Europe" *International Herald Tribune*, 16 September 1996, 17.
38. Ibid.
39. Anne Swardson, "Korean Unrest Casts A Shadow at OECD", *International Herald Tribune*, 20 January 1997, 1.
40. Don Kirk, "*Chaebol* Prevail in Seoul's Labor-Reform Plan" *International Herald Tribune*, 7-8 December 1996, 16.
41. Robert L. Downen, *Of Grave Concern: U.S-Taiwan Relations and the Threshold of the 1980s*, Significant Issues Series 3, no. 4 (Washington, DC: The Center

for Strategic and International Studies, Georgetown University, 1981): 10.

42. *Deng Xiaoping Wenxuan*, vol. 3, (Beijing: Renmin Chubanshe, 1993): 30.

43. Simon Long, *Taiwan to 1993: Politics Versus Prosperity, Special Report No. 1159*, The Economist Intelligence Unit Limited, 1989, 14.

44. John W. Garver, *Foreign Relations of the People's Republic of China* (Englewood Cliffs, NJ: Prentice-Hall, 1993).

45. Harry Harding, *A Fragile Relationship: the United States and China Since 1972* (Washington, DC, The Brookings Institution, 1992): 113.

46. U.S. Senate Committee on the Judiciary, *Taiwan Communiqué and Separation of Powers: Hearings before the Subcommittee on Separation of Powers*, 97th Cong., 2d sess., 17 and 27 September 1982.

47. Ibid., 24–25.

48. *The Honolulu Advertiser*, 12 November 1995, B4.

49. *South China Morning Post*, 4 November 1995, 15.

50. Judith Goldstein and Robert O. Keohane, "Ideas and Foreign Policy: An Analytical Framework" in Judith Goldstein and Robert O. Keohane, eds., *Ideas and Foreign Policy: Beliefs, Institutions, and Political Change* (Ithaca, NY: Cornell University Press, 1993): 12.

51. Thomas B. Gold, *State and Society in the Taiwan Miracle* (New York: M.E. Sharpe, Inc., 1986).

52. Ibid., 17.

53. The groundwork for U.S. policy toward Asia was laid on 16 and 17 September 1958 when J. W. Fulbright was designated to undertake a comprehensive study for the future of U.S. foreign policy under the auspices of the Committee on Foreign Relations. See U.S. Senate Committee on Foreign Relations, *United States Foreign Policy: Asia*, prepared by Conlon Associates Ltd., 86th Cong., 1st sess., 1959, Committee Print 5.

54. Ibid., 22.

55. Chui Kwei Chiang, "Political Attitudes and Organizations, c. 1900–1941" in *A History of Singapore*, eds., Ernest C. T. Chew and Edwin Lee (Singapore: Oxford University Press, 1991): 78–81.

56. The Asia Pacific Centre, *The Markets of Asia/Pacific: Singapore* (Hampshire: Gower Publishing Company Limited, 1981).

57. Yeo Kim Wah and Albert Lau, "From Colonialism to Independence, 1945–1965" *A History of Singapore*, eds., Ernest C. T. Chew and Edwin Lee (Singapore: Oxford University Press, 1991): 124.

58. Ibid.

59. Ibid., 131.

60. Ibid., 147.

61. Joel Krieger, *The Oxford Companion to Politics of the World* (New York: Oxford University Press, 1993): 947.

62. Clark D. Neher, *Southeast Asia in the New International Era* (Boulder, CO: Westview Press, 1991): 14.

63. Krieger, *The Oxford Companion*, 847.

64. Stephan Haggard, *Pathways from the Periphery: The Politics of Growth in the Newly Industrializing Countries* (Ithaca, NY: Cornell University Press, 1990): 146.

65. Cheng Siok Hwa, "Economic Change and Industrialization" in *A History of Singapore*, eds., Ernest C. T. Chew and Edwin Lee (Singapore: Oxford University Press, 1991): 209.

66. Cheah Hock Beng, "Responding to Global Challenges: The Changing Nature of Singapore's Incorporation into the International Economy" in *Singapore Changes*

Guard: Social, Political and Economic Directions in the 1990s, edited by Garry Rodan (New York: St. Martin's Press, 1993): 108.

67. *Economic Development Board Yearbook 1992/1993* (Singapore: EDB, 1993): 66.

68. *Singapore 1988* (Singapore: Information Division: Ministry of Communication and Information, 1988): 72.

69. *Economic Survey of Singapore 1994* (Singapore: Ministry of Trade and Industry, 1995): 7.

Part Three

U.S. Market Augmentation Policy toward China

5

The Cold War Syndrome
and China's Isolation

*The internal changes taking place currently in
most countries of southeast Asia, as well as the
increasing awareness of their elites of the real
nature of communism, are intensifying their hope
that they will be aided by the United States
in solving their problems.[1]*
—U.S. Committee on Foreign Relations

Introduction

The Communist takeover of China in 1949 gave rise to a conceptual as well as operational change in U.S. policy toward China. Moreover, so-called cold war relations were also intensified by Mao Zedong's ideological as well as tactical isolation policy. The major focuses of this chapter will cover the height of the cold war and the isolation policy during the Mao era. This chapter is divided into three parts. In the first part, I will discuss the general atmosphere during the cold war when Sino-American relations were marked by fear. Second, in terms of foreign relations, I will analyze U.S. policy toward China in terms of a strategic triangle which will explain the tenuous relations among the United States, China, and the Soviet Union. Finally, the notion of Mao's conceptual and practical policies will be understood by an analysis of his own work and reports from that area.

The Cold War Syndrome—Fear

Relations between the United States and China were seldom free from hostility. More often than not they were locked in the trap of a "security dilemma,"[2] which was a predicament generated by the continuous mistrust and fear between them.[3] Their relations in the 1950s and 1960s were characterized by the contrast in their perceptions of each other. When China sided with the Soviet Union during the 1950s, its relations with the United States reached a nadir. According to Robert Jervis, "one state's gain in security often inadvertently threatens others."[4] Thus, the Communist takeover of mainland China and subsequent one-sided policy doubled the intensity of fear in the United States government.

Actually, the cloud of fear and uncertainty was earlier highlighted by George F. Kennan in an astonishing article entitled "The Sources of Soviet Conduct" which appeared in *Foreign Affairs* in 1947.[5] As Thucydides observed: "…when the element of fear is present, we fall short of our ideal."[6] The same logic applied to U.S. relations with China, especially before the normalization of Nixon's visit in 1972.

The thrust of cold war strategy, which denoted an important phase in the international political economy,[7] was backed by a sufficient amount of economic endowments in the United States. If U.S. foreign policy objectives were defined in terms of the containment of communism during the cold war, especially between 1949 and 1971, the instrument of its policy was clearly the arms race between the East and the West. It was not an accident that the United States was a leader in the inauguration of the cold war "congregation." The United States was the only power which could initiate the move towards cold war. The diminishing power of the United Kingdom after 1945, the acceleration of socialist movements in the East, the emergence of Communist China in 1949 in particular, and the expansion of the Soviet Union after 1945, all helped to escalate the cold war.[8] The adoption of a more radical and hostile foreign policy towards socialist "liberation" strongly characterized George Kennan's aforementioned article.

To facilitate containment, according to Robert McNamara, former defense secretary in the Kennedy administration, there appeared to be a series of process and preparation. The *mechanism* is detailed as follows:

> By the close of 1955 this system of interlocking alliances had grown to include the Rio Treaty in the Western hemisphere, NATO in Europe, SEATO and ANZUS in the Far East, and the bilateral mutual defense agreements with Korea, Japan, the Republic of China and the Philippines. Altogether, more than fifty sovereign nations bound themselves together in an effort to defend their freedom and prevent the further extension of Communist influence and hegemony through subversion and aggression.[9]

Subsequently, the escalation of fear was further reinforced by the expansion of the Soviet Union in Eastern Europe and the Communists' victory over the Nationalists. This escalation will take us to the next section to investigate the strategic relations among the United States, the Soviet Union, and China in the atmosphere of the cold war.

The Strategic Triangle

As a conceptual tool, the strategic triangle has been used widely to analyze foreign relations among the United States, China, and the Soviet Union during the cold war. Scholars such as John G. Stoessinger, Lowell Dittmer, Roman Kolkowicz, and Min Chen applied the concept in either different perspectives or under a specific periods of time.[10] In a nutshell, the strategic triangle relationship can be described as "playing oneself off against another." As can be seen from figure 5.1, the triangular relationship is most commonly used to analyze their meandering foreign policies.

The direction of relations, however, was indicated by the change of perceptions toward one another in different time periods. The following analysis will discuss the U.S. perception of the Soviet Union and China during a delicate time in the late 1940s and early 1950s, respectively. Then, I will analyze China's relations with the Soviet Union in the 1950s and 1960s. In retrospect, both the United States and China's so-called strategic relations toward the Soviet Union were proven to be relatively short, which then left ample latitude for the opportunity of normalization between the United States and China, realized in the Nixon visit.

FIGURE 5.1
The Triangular System

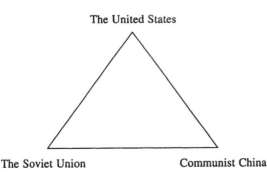

The U. S. Perception of the Soviet Union

The short phase of cooperation right after World War II between the United States and the Soviet Union was disappointing because the strategic cooperation during this period was soon replaced by U.S. hostility toward Soviet expansion in Germany between 1948–1949. In his memoirs, Harry S. Truman details how the Berlin Blockade was gradually built by the relentless expansion of the Soviet Union. He complained that "The Russians on their part; seemed determined to treat their zone of Germany virtually as if it was Soviet conquered territory."[11] In fact, as soon as the Soviet representatives "walked out on the Allied Control Council," the Soviet Union had already prepared for the seizure of Berlin. To further facilitate the division of Berlin, the Soviet Union began to check "all U.S. personnel passing through their zone for identification and would inspect all freight shipments..."[12] Moreover, the Soviets opposed the currency reform initiated by the United States. On 30 November 1948, the Soviet Union occupied the Berlin city council, which signified the completion of the division of Berlin.[13]

The U.S. perception of the Soviet Union completely changed. In addition to the prophetic article written by George F. Kennan in 1947, the U.S. expression of fear of the Soviet Union was addressed further by Dean Acheson, then secretary of state, on 16 March 1950 during a speech delivered at the University of California at Berkeley.[14] The charge was depicted as follows:

> But the Soviet leaders know and the world knows with what genuine disappointment and concern the people of this country were brought to the realization that the wartime collaboration between the major allies was not to be the beginning of [a] happier and freer era in the association between the peoples of the Soviet Union and other peoples.[15]

The U.S. Perception of China

The U.S. perception of China was a combination of fear of the spread of communism and the change in perception of American decision makers toward the world economy. Immediately after World War II, Roosevelt was interested in beginning strategic relations with the National government of China because "the resulting cold war pitted competing blocs of antagonistic states against each other, slowly inducing the United States to see that China's strategic location and market potential could actually make it a useful partner."[16] Nevertheless, as mentioned earlier in the Introduction, the U.S. perception of the National government of China completely changed when it saw the truth about the failure of China's National government. *The China White Paper* prepared by Dean Acheson, then secretary of state, demonstrated that "The unfortunate but inescapable fact is that the ominous result of the civil war in China was beyond the control of the government of the United States."[17] Actually, the decision was made also from the perception of the obvious expansion of the Soviet Union, a clear and present danger to all Europe.

Increasing U.S. fear of communism was further reinforced by McCarthyism. More significantly, before the United States could strive for a corresponding foreign policy in reaction to the then newly established PRC, Congress was overwhelmed by Senator Joseph R. McCarthy's accusation during the hearing held between 8 March and 28 June 1950 that ten officials had connection to the Communists in one way or another. Their activities, as charged, greatly affected U.S. foreign policymakers.[18] This incident caused political outcry in the United States. Not only did it spark a great debate in Congress, but also indicated that the atmosphere of the U.S. government toward communism was skeptical, alert, suspicious, and unprepared.

According to the study done by Seyom Brown, the Berlin blockade between 1948–1949 only explained half of the reason why the implementation of the containment policy was swiftly accepted during the Truman administration. The rest came from the Communist victory over China.[19] The substantial ingredients of military operation in the containment policy was written in NSC-68,[20] which was further initiated by the immediate course of the break-out of the Korean War in 1950. The participation of China in the Korean War resulted in a U.S. trade embargo on nearly every kind of good that was exported to China. When the war escalated in 1952, the embargo was also practiced by the allies of the United States, including Japan.[21] As suggested by the early analysis of triangular relations, the loss of trade from the United States was quickly offset by strategic relations between China and the Soviet Union. For example, the total trade volume between China and the Soviet Union between 1950–59 was 413.16 billion, comprising 47.8 percent of China's total trade.[22] The notion of strategy here represented by China's timely relations with the Soviet Union. The following section will survey how and to what extent their relations were maintained.

China's Perception of the Soviet Union

China's overall perception of the Soviet Union was heavily shaped by the ideological inclination of Chairman Mao. The aftermath of the establishment of the PRC in 1949 marked a turning point in the political and economic development of the PRC in the following two decades. In striving for socialist development, Mao decided to ally with the Soviet Union in an attempt to counterbalance Japanese intimidation and the influence of the United States.[23] Their cooperation resulted in the signing of the Treaty of Friendship, Alliance, and Mutual Assistance between the Soviet Union and the People's Republic of China on 14 February 1950. This treaty embodied a comprehensive bilateral cooperation in diplomatic, economic, military, and political collaboration. For example, the granting of U.S. $300,000,000 to China helped enormously in the facilitation of heavy industrial development.[24] All of sudden, their early relations were characterized by an embracive cooperation in different sectors of the economy and across various programs. To name but a few, more than 10,800 Soviet technical experts were dispatched to China in the 1950s, over 250 to 300 large industrial projects were built in China with the assistance of the Soviet Union and over 1,500 Chinese technicians were trained in the Soviet Union.[25] Primer Li Peng was among those trained in the Soviet Union. In the late 1950s, the Soviet supply of plants and factory equipment, in monetary terms, accounted for $2,000 million.[26]

Nevertheless, the unprecedented diplomatic triumph of the PRC with the help of the Soviet Union undermined many hidden discrepancies between these two giant socialist states. In essence, those differences and problems, on the one hand, reinforced the stability of their future foreign relations. On the other hand, the synthesis of their foreign relations fostered later reabsorption with the world economy after Nixon's visit.

The underlying differences between China and the Soviet Union surfaced in the early 1950s over the issues of Kao Kang, a Chinese Communist leader. Although no concrete evidence corroborated the secret relations between Kao Kang and the Soviet Union, it had been revealed that Stalin had made direct communication with Kao Kang behind the then paramount leader, Mao Zedong.[27] Later, more specifically, during a speech delivered at the Second Plenary Session of the Eighth Central Committee of the Communist Party of China on 15 November 1956, Mao openly identified Kao Kang as "having illicit relations with foreign countries," obviously implying the Soviet Union.[28]

Second, the schism between China and the Soviet Union first appeared after Nikita Sergeyevich Khrushchev's de-Stalinization speech on 25 February 1956 during a closed session of the twentieth Communist Party of the Soviet Union (CPSU) Congress.[29] Mao denounced Khrushchev's criticism of the reliance on heavy industry in national development. Mao then went on and commented that Khrushchev had deviated so much that he was deemed beyond reprieve: not only had he abandoned Leninism and class struggle but he also believed in the parliamentary model of state development.[30] Mao would never agree to a policy which did not complement his socialist ideology.

The approach of the 1960s saw the climax of Sino-Soviet confrontation. After the Cuban Missile Crisis of 1962,[31] China had begun its attack on the Soviet Union under the guise of "adventurism."[32] Their antagonism increased when the Soviet Union signed the Limited Test Ban Treaty with the United States and Britain in July 1963. Following suit was the exchange of letters between the Chinese Communist Party (CCP) and CPSU during late 1963 and 1964. Those letters, known as the "nine-comments," sent by the CCP to the CPSU vehemently unearthed the differences, grievances, and complaints about the Soviet Union.[33] For example, the letter sent to the CPSU on 20 February 1964 indicated that China was upset about the CPSU's secret letter to the other fraternal parties as a way to condemn China.[34] The subsequent letters also pointed to the conflicts between China and the Soviet Union over the various issues including territory, aid, and trading activities.[35] The sensitivity of Mao and his perception toward the Soviet Union in undertaking such activities, imperatively urged him to foster an entire break-up of bilateral relations with the Soviet Union. The most encompassing danger on the brink of military conflict between China and the Soviet Union took place over the disputed island of Chenpao near the River Ussuri in March 1969. In an official statement, China declared that "Chenpao Island is China's territory and the Chenpao Island incident was deliberately provoked by the Soviet government"[36] The escalation of war eventually ameliorated when Premier of the State Council Chou En-lai had a "frank" talk with Kosygin, chairman of the Council of Ministers of the Soviet Union.[37] Nevertheless, the foreign relations between them never returned to the level of the 1950s.

The isolation of Chinese development in such circumstances, after the break-up with its sole alliance, the Soviet Union, continued to the extent of abandonment and further desertion of the international economy. The Great Leap Forward and the Cultural Revolution dramatized and crystallized the futility of China's segregation from the world economy and the dissipation of energy in a self-destructive struggle. Facilitated by Mao's original works and ample newspaper resources, the following sections will shed light on the domestic part of Chinese isolation.

Mao's Policies of Isolation

The revolutionary ideas of Mao Zedong and the effective isolation policy of China from the world market economy in the 1950s and 1960s collectively disengaged China from a global economic take-off. Mao's ideological orthodoxy with respect to the belief of continuous revolution and conflict enmeshed China's economy into an abyss of economic underdevelopment. For example, development policies such as the Great Leap Forward and upheavals such as the Cultural Revolution disrupted economic development. In terms of foreign policy, Mao's communist ideology and concept of international revolution naturally pushed him to "lean to one side,"[38] to the former Soviet Union for psychological as well as physical support either to collaborate or confederate under socialism.[39] On the contrary, China's relations with the United States were reciprocated by the U.S. containment policy for fear that its socialist movement might spread relentlessly throughout the world. The embargo that the United States put on Communist China was regarded by Rosemary Foot as "the primary economic purpose of delaying the country's modernization and thus the development of its military capacity."[40] This centrifugal effect certainly delayed China's development process. Nevertheless, the personal traits of Mao also played a substantial role in keeping China from the international society.

In other words, Mao's idiosyncrasies in the face of translating socialism into an operational strategy that would propel the country forward actually hindered economic development, especially engagement with the world political economy. Strategic and practical imperatives thus pushed China toward the former Soviet Union not only for economic reasons but also for communist affinity. Coupled with the disasters of the Great Leap Forward and the Cultural Revolution, China's political economy under Mao's control was highly segregated from the world economic developmental process. The following sections will detail these processes.

Mao emphasizes conflict and revolution. His idea of war and the tactics of guerrilla warfare culminated in his conflict theory. Nevertheless, Stuart R. Schram argues that "Mao's blind spots reflect not only his own personality and experience, but certain weaknesses of Marxism as a system. By temperament, Mao is impatient with the routine and technical character of modern economic activity."[41] The emphasis on socialist transformation and revolution threw the whole society into internal chaos while functionally distancing itself from the world market economy. The anachronism between Mao's military intelligence and revolutionary ideas in government administration resulted in the underdevelopment and antagonistic nature of China in the 1950s and 1960s. Albeit, the end of civil war in 1949 did not terminate his encompassing revolutionary ideas. The basic principle of war, Mao asserted, is "to strive to the utmost to preserve one's own strength and destroy that of the enemy."[42] A pioneer in the field of guerrilla warfare, Mao's intelligence in the empirical warfare experience was captured in his idea of transforming guerrilla warfare into a mobile war during the Japanese invasion in the late 1930s. As he points out:

> Since the war is protracted and ruthless, it is possible for the guerrilla units to undergo the necessary steeling and gradually to transform themselves into regular forces, so that their mode of operations is gradually regularized and guerrilla warfare develops into mobile warfare.[43]

Mao's strategies in warfare earned him the country by expelling China's Nationalists—the Kuomintang (KMT) to Taiwan. Nevertheless, encapsulated in his revolutionary mode of economic development, Mao's passion for revolution perpetuated by means of the administrative and governmental development of the PRC in the following decades. His belief in contradiction inevitably dichotomized Chinese domestic growth in the way of socialist transformation and the bourgeois capitalist economic development of the rest of the world.[44] To put it bluntly, the whole logic of Mao was to "exterminate the bourgeoisie and capitalism in China."[45] Here, it can be understood why China's economy in the 1950s and 1960s was isolated from the world market economy not only in terms of physical trade and cooperation but also in the more fundamental differentiation of the mentality toward development. Actually, the idea of exterminating capitalism was not only exercised domestically. Mao's propaganda was also meant to spread throughout the rest of the world. He exclaimed that "Our aim is to exterminate capitalism, obliterate it from the face of the earth and make it a thing of the past."[46] The confrontation between China and the world economy, thereafter, accelerated as a defensive approach to the

Chinese economic growth strategy became an offensive tactic aimed at world society. In such circumstances, China basically disengaged itself from the world market economy, which was at that time, dominated by the hegemonic power of the United States.

To further alienate China from the world market, Mao's idea of China's industrialization process depended on the internal agricultural force and the development of heavy industries.[47] It paved the way for strengthening cooperation with the former Soviet Union; socialist ties intended to connect all socialist states.[48]

The Great Leap Forward (1958–1960)

Mao's belief in conflict and revolution not only gave rise to intimate cooperation with the U.S.S.R but eventually later conflict and confrontation. The results of using ideological incentives to run the government administration and industrial management led to serious famine and human catastrophe during and after the Great Leap Forward (1958–60). According to Roderick MacFarquhar, one of the major contributing factors to the Great Leap Forward was the difference of opinion between Mao and Khrushchev over the conceptual and tactical ways to assess and realize a socialist revolution during the fortieth anniversary of the Bolshevik Revolution held in Moscow in late 1957.[49] Moreover, after Mao made an inspection tour in Hangchow and Nanning, the ideas and theoretical assumptions of the Great Leap Forward gradually precipitated and later were put forward in the Sixth Articles about work methods.[50]

The launch of the Great Leap Forward followed the Report to the Second Session of the Eighth Party Congress on 5 May 1958 by Liu Shaoqi as a reaction to Soviet de-Stalinization and capitalist exploitation.[51] Hence, the intensity of the Great Leap Forward increased after the Central Committee's Decision on the People's Communes of 29 August 1958 and the Politburo's simultaneous call for doubling the output of iron and steel. As argued by James Wang, the Great Leap Forward centered on the combination of labor-intensive production methods and the widespread use of communes to enhance the production of industrial as well as agricultural products.[52] The belief in self-perpetuation, enthusiasm, and unscientific modes of production inherently embodied the elements of failure. The lack of competition, material incentive, and comparison with the world economy only resulted in unnecessary waste, human catastrophe, and exaggerated reports and statistical results, especially in the agricultural sector and steel production. The following cases offer a glimpse of newspaper reports that covered those invented and polluted cases found in some localities, a phenomenon that happened regularly in those days.

Falsifying Reports and Cases in Hebei and Yunan

At the height of the Great Leap Forward, most newspaper articles and reports covered two major items: agriculture and industry, particularly steel. The editorials of *Yunan Ribao*, for instance, from May to June 1959, continuously reported spectacular results in paddy and rice growing and fabulous improvement in steel manufacturing.[53] For example, in terms of steel production, an article revealed that furnace no. 1 of the Kunming steel plant produced quality iron in twenty-three out of twenty-nine days.[54] In addition, as reported, the rate of paddy and rice production was one acre per day among all of the Yunan provinces.[55] In order to glorify the domestic achievements of the Great Leap Forward and demonize capitalist states, overseas news would sometimes be editorially manipulated as a demonstration of propaganda. Stories about millions of poor people living in shanty towns and squatter areas in New York City were not uncommon.[56]

While the provincial newspaper reported spurious, exaggerated and illogical results of agriculture and industrial development, the national newspaper, *Renmin Ribao*, drew attention to world affairs in which conflicts could be found among the developed and developing countries. For instance, on 6 March 1962, the editor of *Renmin Ribao* blamed the high growth rate of Japan on exploitation by the state and entrepreneurs. The high savings rate, a characteristic of Japanese culture, was also criticized as a tool of exploitation.[57] Ironically, the function of the state, the tripartite relations among the government, business, and politicians and the relations between savings rates and investment, on the contrary, were major factors that contributed to Japanese economic growth.[58]

Some spurious reports were also found in Hebei. In 1958, a newspaper illustrated that people used only two days to complete the reforestation of 16,000 acres of land.[59] The quantum speed of afforestation, as a reaction to the central authority, only led to unbelievable figures. For example, on 10 March 1958, the central government set a target of 20,000,000 acres for the afforestation program. In only seventeen days, each municipal witnessed enormous results in finishing the job. The following table, taken from *Hebei Ribao*, details the amazing pace of afforestation that took place.

TABLE 5.1
Afforestation in Hebei Province (March 1958)

Areas	Finished Areas (acres)	Percentage as Planned	Trees Planted (number)	Percentage as Planned
Total	6,193,988	31	437,943,902	69.4
Chengde	206,170	5.1	36,709,018	36.7
Tangshan	131,535	6.8	5,446,437	12.3
Dongcheng	211,375	15.6	26,360,000	43.2
Zhangjiakou	1,187,093	29.6	18,069,963	44.1
Baoding	340,359	12.6	47,000,000	76.0
Shijiazhuang	1,279,422	47.4	51,815,779	45.8
Xingtai	1,681,982	98.9	72,585,923	180.9
Handan	1,080,000	108.0	89,000,000	209.4
Tianjin	24,576	9.1	8,729,199	22.0
Cangzhou	51,046	32.0	79,467,241	96.5
Qinhuangdao	—	—	—	—
Zhangjiakou City	—	—	—	—
Tangshan City	—	—	562,775	98.8
Shijiazhuang City	430	2.9	527,567	17.4
Handan City	—	—	—	—
Baoding City	—	—	1,670,000	75.9

Source: *Hebei Ribao*, 29 March 1958, 1.

To accomplish the job in such little time revealed nothing but the fact that people were unaware about the illogic of the information. Nor did they have the scientific knowledge to judge the authenticity of the data. What they relied on was the ideological indoctrination of Chairman Mao. Invented data such as the above-mentioned might result in people's loss of confidence in the government. These primitive methods of estimating production and growth were actually destructive and disastrous to the economy. For instance, untrained and uneducated peasants were used as advisers for irrigation projects.[60] Government officials also believed in not using concrete and steel when building dams and dykes.[61] A village proverb found in a newspaper was illustrative of the way in which passionate enthusiasm was embodied in the people's interpretation of agricultural development.

A Village Proverb (from *Hebei Ribao*, 6 March 1958, 2)

> Sweet potato taken from village is like a horse,
> a gallop jumps to 1962
> Each household grows 1.8 acres sweet potatoes,
> enough for eating, wearing and spending.
> Each acre uses 20 carts fertilizer,
> with returns of 10 thousand jin....

The nature of the Great Leap Forward was aimed at the acceleration of national production by using human resources in a passionate and sentimental way, instead of relying on rational and calculated management and administrative procedures. Without management skills and implementation knowledge, the communes—the relatively decentralized collective units—were only a loosely "divided policy-making system" that had serious problems coordinating a collective effort.[62] Moreover, the lack of technological know-how and even the common sense of agricultural and industrial development did more harm than good. The implicit and explicit problems of the Great Leap Forward, together with floods and famine in 1959 and 1960, led to the entire collapse and destruction of China's national economy. Remarking on the Great Leap Forward, Jean-Luc Domenach contended that "Not only did the Great Leap Forward produce a terrible catastrophe, but its political formulation and even more the nature of the Chinese Communist regime made the catastrophe inevitable."[63] In fact, the catastrophe did not stop right after the Great Leap Forward. Another period of political and economic chaos, the Cultural Revolution, began soon after in the 1960s.

Cultural Revolution

By a wide margin, the Cultural Revolution witnessed the disillusionment of the socialist dream in the realistic intransigence of Communist China's politics. More importantly, it facilitated a huge drawback in the economic sector as well as in the political sphere. The predicament of Chinese socialist development reached its lowest peak during the Cultural Revolution (1966–1976). As a formal government policy, the Cultural Revolution was launched on 8 August 1966 after the eleventh session of the Eighth Central Committee.[64]

The Cultural Revolution, as a complex political and social incident, has very "often been represented in the West as a struggle between pragmatism and radical ideology."[65] Nevertheless, studies of the Cultural Revolution have fragmented into various disciplines. To analyze the historical trajectory of *The Origins of Cultural Revolution*, Roderick MacFarquhar focuses on the macro-history of Chinese Communist development, which eventually engendered the Cultural Revolution.[66] Others, such as Gao Yuan, who served as a Red Guard during the height of the Revolution, gives an account of the personal experience of his day-to-day experiences as well as the development of the Revolution.[67] In addition, the recent study of the Cultural Revolution by Shaoguang Wang gives a political diagnosis, using the theoretical analysis of a rational choice model to study the masses.[68] No matter how we interpret the Cultural Revolution, as concluded by William A. Joseph, this chaotic decade has become and will continue to be a political, social, and economic trauma because "there are deep psychological scars that individual Chinese will bear for life and social wounds that will not heal for generations."[69]

Specific reasons contributed to the relentless speed and unprecedented extent of the Cultural Revolution. First, in terms of foreign relations, the withdrawal of Soviet economic advisers and assistance in the early 1960s imperatively pushed China into an embarrassed and awkward situation.[70] With limited alternatives, the yield to extreme socialist thinking and political chaos occurred.

Second, the origin of the Cultural Revolution might be traced to Mao's dismay over a series of plays, novels, and articles that appeared in the early 1960s. The play, *Hai Rui's Dismissal from Office*, for example, was considered to be critical of Mao's mismanagement during the Great Leap Forward.[71] And, finally, for purely practical reasons, the Cultural Revolution was also a power struggle between Mao and higher- echelon officials[72] such as Liu Shaoqi and Lin Biao of the Communist party. Clashes and antagonisms between Mao and Liu Shaoqi were further exposed in the newspapers. Headlines such as THOROUGH CRITICISM OF LIU SHAOQI AS TRAITOR AND THIEF OF ANTI-REVOLUTIONARY REVISIONISM appeared frequently in the major newspapers such as the *People's Daily*.[73] On 16 May 1969, the criticisms of Liu Shaoqi pointed out his belief in experts and professionalism in factory management and administration.[74] In the turbulent years of submission to ideological purity, the belief in experts was not considered to be politically correct. In a similar fashion, heavy criticism of Lin Biao also occurred in local newspapers in 1973. The anachronistic juxtapositions of Lin's criticism and the improvement of agriculture and porcelain only served to reveal the articles' underlying theme: this was a struggle for power, with Mao obviously monopolizing the forum.[75]

The above case reveals that, during the Cultural Revolution, the people's strength and energy were wastefully absorbed and gradually channeled into domestic contention. The means and modes of production were governed not by the logic of market forces and incentives but by frenzied ideological and political indoctrination. In fact, the problem of Chinese development under pure ideological incentives was clearly stated in a study carried out by Barry M. Richman in 1966 of the Chinese industrial and management sectors. He reached a pessimistic conclusion and, actually, a prediction of the hopelessly extreme doctrine of socialism in the managerial and industrial sectors if material incentives and managerial methods were undermined.[76] Moreover, his concluding remarks clearly highlighted the gist of the study and also provided hindsight into the way in which China had become involved in the world economy. He mentioned that:

> If Communist China does ever evolve into a truly first-rate power, it would appear that some of the more important aspects of pure Maoist-Marxist ideology would have to be abandoned, or at least greatly compromised in the process.[77]

Apart from the problems found in industrial and managerial development, the economy of China during the Cultural Revolution was also a disaster. From 1965 to 1975, the average annual growth rate of grain output per capita was 1.1 percent,[78] while the growth rate of the population during this period was 2.4 percent.[79] One can imagine the hardship that people suffered and the fragility of the political economy of China at that time. The death of Mao on 9 September 1976 not only represented a termination of his political life, but was actually a historical juncture for China. In a sense, Mao's death allowed China the freedom to begin to reshape its course of development from domestic political struggle to economic openness and adaptation to the world market economy.

Conclusion

This chapter began by exploring the trajectory of strategic relations among the United States, China, and the Soviet Union. As mentioned earlier, neither relations between the United States and the Soviet Union nor relations between China and the Soviet Union represented genuine cooperation. By looking at the plight of the domestic economy depicted above during the Mao era, a new course of development seemed imperative for China. Policies based on economic development are a rational outcome not only for decision makers but also for the entire nation.

In addition, the 1970s saw the historical change of the world economy and a change in U.S. foreign policy. The next chapter will, therefore, analyze how the world political economy facilitated a change in U.S. policy toward China.

Notes

1. U.S. Senate Committee on Foreign Relations, *United States Foreign Policy: Asia*, 86th Cong., 1st sess., 1959, Committee Print, 82.
2. There are two types of security dilemma, the "inadvertent security dilemma" and "deliberate security dilemma." Although their aims are different, the result of both could be destructive. They break the cooperative possibility between states and produce further hostility between them. For a theoretical understanding of this concept, see Nicholas J. Wheeler and Ken Booth, "The Security Dilemma" in John Baylis and N.J. Rengger, eds., *Dilemma of World Politics: International Issues in a Changing World* (Oxford: Clarendon Press, 1992): 29–60.
3. Ibid., 38.
4. Robert Jervis, "Cooperation Under the Security Dilemma," *World Politics* 30, no. 2 (1978): 170.
5. Instead of using his real name, he used "X" as a pseudonym. See X, "The Sources of Soviet Conduct," in *Foreign Affairs* 25, no. 4 (July 1947): 566–82. The argument in this article about the internationalization of socialism was adopted by the government as the major foreign policy orientation, which directly led to the precipitation of the cold war. See also Stephen E. Ambrose, *Rise to Globalism: American Foreign Policy Since 1938*, 7th. ed., (London: Penguin Books, 1993): 95–96.
6. Thucydides, *History of The Peloponnesian War*, translated by Rex Warner (London: Penguin Books, 1972): 105.
7. Robert A. Isaak, *International Political Economy: Managing World Economic Change* (Englewood Cliffs, NJ: Prentice-Hall International, Inc., 1991): 44–54.
8. Robert J. Bresler, "The Origins and Development of the Cold War, 1945–58" in Ronald Barston, ed., *International Politics Since 1945* (London: Edward Elgar, 1991): 1–17.
9. Robert S. McNamara, *The Essence of Security: Reflections in Office* (New York: Harper and Row, Publishers, 1968): 5. SEATO is an acronym for Southeast Asia Treaty Organization and ANZUS refers to Australia, New Zealand, and the U.S. Defense Pact. See Joel Krieger, ed., *The Oxford Companion to Politics of the World* (New York: Oxford University Press, 1993): 847–848 and Gerald Segal, *The World Affairs Companion: The Essential One-Volume Guide to Global Issues*, revised ed., (London: Simon and Schuster, 1993): 199 for details.
10. John G. Stoessinger depicted each of their interrelations under the framework of international politics. See John G. Stoessinger, *Nations at Dawn: China, Russia, and America*, 6th ed., (New York: McGraw-Hall, Inc., 1994). Lowell Dittmer applied the strategic concept in a game model. Lowell Dittmer, "The Strategic Triangle: An Elementary Game-Theoretical Analysis" *World Politics* 33, no. 4 (July 1981): 485–515. Roman Kolkowics, nevertheless, focused on the relations between the United States and the Soviet Union. See Roman Kolkowicz, "Strategic Parity and Beyond: Soviet Perspectives" *World Politics* 23, no. 3 (April 1971): 431–451. Min Chen put forth the concept in the specific context of the

Indochinese Wars. See Min Chen, *The Strategic Triangle and Regional Conflicts: Lessons from the Indochina Wars* (Boulder, CO: Lynne Rienner Publishers, 1992).

11. Harry S. Truman, *Memoirs by Harry S. Truman* (New York: A Signet Book, 1956): 146.
12. Ibid., 147.
13. Ibid., 155.
14. Department of State, *American Foreign Policy 1950–1955, Basic Documents, Vol. II* (Washington, DC: Department of State, 1957): 1928.
15. Ibid., 1934.
16. Nancy Bernkopf Tucker, "China and America: 1941–1991" *Foreign Affairs* 70, no. 5 (Winter 1991/92): 78.
17. Department of State, *The China White Paper, August 1949* (Stanford, CA: Stanford University Press, 1967): XVI.
18. Congressional Quarterly Service, *China and U.S. Far East Policy, 1945–1967* (Washington, DC: Congressional Quarterly Service, 1967): 14.
19. Seyom Brown, *The Faces of Power: United States Foreign Policy from Truman to Clinton*, 2d ed., (New York: Columbia University Press, 1994): 36.
20. NSC-68 refers to the name of files prepared by the National Security Council. See ibid., 37–39.
21. Rosemary Foot, *The Practice of Power: US Relations with China Since 1949* (Oxford: Clarendon Press, 1995): 53.
22. Ibid., 56.
23. Harold C. Hinton, ed., *Government and Politics in Revolutionary China: Selected Documents, 1949–1979* (Wilmington, DE: Scholarly Resources Ins., 1982): 8.
24. Ibid., 10.
25. A. Doak Barnett, *China and the Major Powers in East Asia* (Washington, DC: The Brookings Institution, 1977): 28.
26. G. F. Hudson, Richard Lowenthal, and Roderick MacFarquhar, *The Sino-Soviet Dispute* (London: The China Quarterly, 1961): 37.
27. A. Doak Barnett, *China*, 30.
28. *Selected Works of Mao Zedong*, vol. 5 (Peking: Foreign Languages Press, 1977): 340.
29. John W. Garver, *Foreign Relations of the People's Republic of China* (Englewood-Cliffs, NJ: Prentice-Hall, 1993): 125.
30. *Selected Works of Mao Zedong*, vol. 5 (Peking: Foreign Languages Press, 1977): 341.
31. See Graham T. Allison, *Essence of Decision: Explaining the Cuban Missile Crisis* (New York: HarperCollins, 1971) for the details of the incident that happened in October 1962.
32. *Peking Review*, 6 September 1963, 14.
33. The first comment entitled: "The Origin and Development of the Differences between the Leadership of the C.P.S.U. and Ourselves" and the last one named "On Khrushohev's Phoney Communism and Its Historical Lessons for the World." See A. Doak Barnett, *China and the Major Powers in East Asia* (Washington, DC: The Brookings Institution, 1977): 348, note 81.
34. William E. Griffith, *Sino-Soviet Relations 1964–1965* (Cambridge, MA: The MIT Press, 1967): 173–174.
35. Ibid., 181–190.
36. Harold C. Hinton, ed., *Government and Politics in Revolutionary China: Selected Documents, 1949–1979* (Wilmington, DE: Scholarly Resources Ins., 1982): 303.

37. Ibid., 308.
38. A. Doak Barnett, *China and the Major Powers in East Asia* (Washington, DC: The Brookings Institution, 1977): 21.
39. *Selected Works of Mao Zedong*, vol. 5 (Peking: Foreign Languages Press, 1977): 17.
40. Rosemary Foot, *The Practice of Power*, 54.
41. Stuart R. Schram, *The Political Thought of Mao Zedong* (New York: Frederick A. Praeger Publisher, 1963): 83.
42. *Selected Works of Mao Zedong*, vol. 2 (Peking: Foreign Languages Press, 1967): 1.
43. Ibid., 107.
44. *Selected Works of Mao Zedong*, vol. 5 (Peking: Foreign Languages Press, 1977): 212 and 305.
45. Ibid., 214.
46. Ibid.
47. Ibid., 419.
48. Ibid., 421.
49. Roderick MacFarquhar, *The Origins of the Cultural Revolution, vol. 2: The Great Leap Forward 1958–60* (Columbia: RIIA and Columbia University Press, 1983): 7.
50. Ibid., 20.
51. Harold C. Hinton, *Government and Politics*, 73.
52. James C. F. Wang, *Contemporary Chinese Politics: An Introduction*, 4th ed. (Englewood Cliffs, NJ: Prentice-Hall International, Inc., 1992): 15.
53. *Yunan Ribao*, 1 May 1959 to 30 June 1959.
54. *Yunan Ribao*, 5 June 1959, 1.
55. *Yunan Ribao*, 18 June 1959, 1.
56. *Yunan Ribao*, 28 June 1959, 4.
57. *Renmin Ribao*, 6 March 1962, 3.
58. See Kozo Yamamura and Yasukichi Yasuba, eds., *The Political Economy of Japan, vol. 1. The Domestic Transformation* (Stanford, CA: Stanford University Press, 1987).
59. *Hebei Ribao*, 3 March 1958, 1.
60. *Hebei Ribao*, 21 March 1958, 1.
61. *Hebei Ribao*, 8 March 1958, 3.
62. David M. Lampton, "Health Policy during the Great Leap Forward" *The China Quarterly*, no. 60 (October/ December 1974): 698.
63. Jean-Luc Domenach, *The Origins of the Great Leap Forward: The Case of One Chinese Province*, trans. A. M. Berrett, (Boulder, CO: Westview Press, 1995): 167.
64. James C. F. Wang, *Contemporary Chinese Politics*, 19.
65. Iain Mclean, ed., *The Concise Oxford Dictionary of Politics* (Oxford: Oxford University Press, 1996): 123.
66. The two volumes of MacFarquhar's *The Origins of the Cultural Revolution* are considered a comprehensive study of this historical incident. See Roderick MacFarquhar, *The Origins of the Cultural Revolution: Contradictions Among the People 1956–1957* (Columbia: Columbia University Press, 1974) and Roderick MacFarquhar, *The Origins of the Cultural Revolution: The Great Leap Forward 1968–1960* (Columbia: Columbia University Press, 1983).
67. Gao Yuan, *Born Red: A Chronicle of the Cultural Revolution* (Stanford, CA: Stanford University Press, 1987).

68. Shaoguang Wang, *Failure of Charisma: The Cultural Revolution in Wuhan* (Hong Kong: Oxford University Press, 1995).
69. Gao Yuan, *Born Red*, xxvii and xxvii.
70. Allen S. Whiting, "The Sino-Soviet Split" in *The Cambridge History of China, Vol. 14, The People's Republic, Part I: The Emergence of Revolutionary China, 1949–1965*, ed. Roderick Macfarquhar and John K. Fairbank (London: Cambridge University Press, 1987): 520.
71. James, C.F. Wang, *Contemporary Chinese Politics*, 20.
72. Gao Yuan, *Born Red*, xvi.
73. From May to June of 1969, for example, the attack of Liu appeared four times in critical, even cursed, full-page articles. See *People's Daily*, May 1969 to June 1969.
74. *People's Daily*, 16 May 1969, 4.
75. *Sichuan Daily*, 6 and 13 October 1973, 2 and 4, respectively.
76. Barry M. Richman, *Industrial Society in Communist China* (New York: Vintage Books, 1969): 914–915.
77. Ibid., 916.
78. Carl Riskin, *China's Political Economy: The Quest for Development Since 1949* (New York: Oxford University Press, 1987): 185.
79. Ibid

6

Nixon's 1972 Visit to China as a Result of Market Forces

That begins with recognition that China has yet to shake the world; its external influence has been comparatively inconsequential since the industrial revolution. Instead, it is the world that has shaken China.[1]

—Bruce Cumings

Introduction

The previous chapter began by examining the atmosphere of fear that affected perceptions between the U.S. and China. Sometimes, viewing this through a cold war haze limited the ways of looking at a particular issue. Some analysts in light of the cold war have very strong explanations for rapprochement between the U.S. and China. Nevertheless, some other scholars had already begun to search for a new perspective towards Sino-American relations.

In 1971, a book entitled *China Trade Prospects and U.S. Policy* was published. Scholars such as Jerome Alan Cohen, Robert F. Dernberger, and John R. Garson proposed a new blueprint to look for some economic reasons or market opportunities between China and the United States at that time.[2] By using economic and legal comparisons, they arrived at a step-by-step trade liberalization policy to open the market of China. Steps included "the complete removal of the embargo on direct and indirect trade in nonstrategic goods; U.S. flag carriers could transport 'nonstrategic' commodities to and from Chinese ports; and remove all restrictions on travel by any U.S. citizen to China and would permit him to purchase commodities and services directly from Chinese within China."[3]

In essence, they intended to draw the attention of the whole government to "what would happen if the U.S. government and businessmen were to offer to assist China in its economic development effort through both trade and aid."[4] This study hinted that a remarkable turning point in their normalization would be based on the market force. As long as they constructed the blueprint for the prospects of Sino-America relations, the rest of the job would depend on the formal diplomatic decision initiated by the U.S. President.

Moreover, 1971 was also the year of the collapse of the gold standard system.[5] President Nixon, on 15 August 1971, announced that the U.S. government could not support the gold-pegged U.S. dollars which were over-valued at that moment. The President Charles de Gaulle of France even questioned the creditworthiness of the United States in the exchange of the same amount of gold with U.S. dollars. The price of gold rose to $65 an ounce (the official price was set at $35 an ounce) on the London market.[6] The U.S. dollar was expected to depreciate. This incident was startling to the international economy. As soon as the United States announced the breakdown of the gold standard, the floating exchange rate system flourished.

Coincidentally, relations between the United States and China dramatically changed from hostility to acceptance. The U.S. table tennis team paid a historical visit to China in 1971. Even Premier Chou En-lai received visiting American table tennis players and told them their visit had "opened [a] new page in relations of Chinese and American people."[7] Following suit, Henry Kissinger, then national security adviser, secretly went to China to lay the groundwork for Nixon's formal visit in 1972. The six-day visit, from 22 February 1972 to 28 February 1972, was concluded by the signing of the Shanghai Communiqué, which paved the way for U.S.-China harmonization in foreign relations. It indicated the first period of normalization between these two great powers after World War II.

This chapter attempts to provide an alternative by interpreting Nixon's visit as the externalization of the international political economy, with the market functioning as the central agency. This chapter will begin with the introduction of some other prevailing cold war arguments of the interpretation of the normalization. They represent the major arguments that dominated the cold war debate. Second, the reinterpretation of Nixon's visit will be studied from the analysis of the congressional hearing held in 1967 that laid the foundation for opting for the market liberalism policy, particularly in the case of wheat-selling, toward the world economy in general and China in particular. Third, this section will explore questions of why Nixon organized his visit to China. The final section surveys the preparations that were made before the launch.

Two Prevailing Cold War Interpretations

The following section will briefly examine two articles published in *Foreign Policy* in 1975 and 1976, respectively.[8] They represent the major perspectives embedded in the spirit of the cold war during that time period. The first point of view represented those who placed emphasis on the strategical reasons of the normalization toward Sino-America relations. The other will investigate the domestic power struggle of China for the justification of the visit.

In the first article, Michael Pillsbury, an analyst from the Rand Corporation, attempted to interpret Nixon's visit by linking Sino-America relations with "military ties".[9] In essence, the strategic wants of China at that time were well represented by his discovery of China's request for U.S. military armaments. By searching for sources available from Russia or the United States, logically, he postulated two tentative, but inspiring explanations of China's strategic wants. A foreign policy initiative to "seek Western military equipment, defense technology, and intelligence?"[10] and "to play upon the conspiratorial instincts of Soviet analysts" became his conclusive education from strategical analysis.[11] The United States, in return, paved the way for further enhancement of diplomatic relations with China by selling weapons, as well as arousing the attention of the Soviet Union in keeping an eye on the Sino-Soviet border.[12] In that circumstance, the whole visit was understood as the externalization of the balancing power of the United States.

In the second article, Roger Glenn Brown argued that the facilitation of Sino-American normalization was influenced predominantly by the internal power struggle. Generally, the clash between the conservatives and the progressives on the opening of China to the United States and the lesser tension over the Sino-Soviet border disputes gave rise to the importance of U.S. normalization with China.[13] In addition, the fall of Lin Biao also accelerated the pace of Sino-American normalization, which meant victory to the prevailing power who supported the normalization.[14]

These arguments represent the realist's interpretation of Nixon's dramatic visit to China. The implications were profound in a sense that triangular relations and the power struggle in the international economy was relatively unchanged in the context of Nixon's visit. Nevertheless, the anatomy of international relations from bilateral or even trilateral relations sometimes undermine the imperative of the international economy.

Between the Lines from Congressional Hearings

As long as the "high politics" played in Vietnam were in its highest stage, the "low politics" of trade and economic activities were also in full swing. The period from 1962 to 1967 was called the Kennedy Round in the GATT negotiation of international trade and tariff reduction. By the end of this round in May 1967, the average reduction of tariffs reached a record 35 percent.[15] Immediately after the conclusion of the Kennedy Round, the Subcommittee on Foreign Economic Policy organized a hearing on "The Future of U.S. Foreign Trade Policy" in July 1967. The purpose of this hearing was described as follows:

> to examine the past, not to find errors, but to take stock and learn our lessons well;
> to try to foresee the changes that are imminent and to direct our efforts accordingly;
> to persuade the United States to dispense with policies that are anachronistic, or which cater to outmoded demands, and to reinforce our efforts to achieve significant and necessary advances in the international commerce of nations, and of the United States in particular;
> to deal plainly with the special interests of our own country in agriculture and industry, while always remembering the primary importance of the general public interest;
> to give our negotiators the basis for firm and flexible bargaining with our trading partners in other countries and through agencies such as GATT; and finally,
> to keep constantly in mind the interdependence of the trading world and the need to maintain its growth and prosperity, which represents for us all the best protection.[16]

Those points presented in the above quotation and many other similar arguments expressed in the hearing demonstrated that the United States should be courageous in opening a new horizon in the area of trade. Such a move not only arrested the tide of the decrease of the United States' unilateral power but also generated an environment governed by the facilitation of the norms of the international economy. The reasons were not only for the benefit of U.S. interests but also for the consideration of the global market economy. Actually, George W. Ball, the former under secretary of state, had bluntly commented that:

> the problem we encounter again and again in our trading relations with the Iron Curtain, or for that matter, even with Red China, is that our producers are denied

the opportunity of making perfectly good sales of their products in the belief that we are hurting the Iron countries by denying them something, when the fact is that they can get these same products elsewhere, and do get them elsewhere. All we are doing is an act of self-flagellation that doesn't advance the American interest.[17]

To be more explicit, he continued by putting forward his idea that even China and the United States could cooperate, even during the height of cold war, in the way of underpinning market forces. He mentions that wheat, as a commodity, can be a starting point in building a market incentive of exchange between the United States and China:

> Now, I would say the same thing with regard to Red China, but with a qualification. The case I was thinking of, specifically, was American wheat. I think it is a terrible shame that we didn't offer our wheat on the market some years ago when Red China was buying from Australia and Canada. The American wheat farmer would have enjoyed a prosperity he has never known in history. The Chinaman got his wheat. He could have bought it just as well from us, and the American farmer would have enjoyed a certain prosperity, and China would have been in the same position, no matter what happened. It seems to me that this was a situation where we let a kind of primitive morality get in the way of practical good sense.[18]

Although Mr. Ball's proposal at this time was a bit outrageous, compared with the battle fought in Vietnam, the gist of his argument could be understood from the Pareto preference, meaning that further exchange of goods can produce a benefit to both parties.[19] In terms of Sino-America relations, his idea gradually aroused attention. Actually, the suggestion that he made earlier was eventually realized after the Nixon's visit. If one looks at the trend of change in the U.S. exportation of wheat and related products to China before and after the Nixon's 1972 visit, one will understand the importance of the market. It also justifies and reinforces Mr. Ball's opinion during the aforementioned hearing held before 1972.

Hence, the unprecedented increase in the exportation of cereal indicates that the reasons behind Nixon's visit could be justified, although not solely, by the market force which, at the height of the cold war, could bridge the ideological gap. However, the strength of the market force could only be revealed in a more systematic and consistent manner after Deng Xiaoping's later policy of economic openness.

The Orchestration of Nixon's Visit

According to John King Fairbank, Nixon's trip to Beijing was considered "a dramatic turn away from cold war confrontation onto the

TABLE 6. 1

U.S. Exportation of Wheat and Maize to China (1971–1978) (in U.S.$1 million)

Year	Wheat	Maize
1971	—	—
1972	64.3	40.3
1973	277.7	132.4
1974	234.0	95.7
1975	—	—
1976	—	—
1977	—	—
1978	250.2	111.7

Source: OECD, Statistics of Foreign Trade, Annual: Tables by Reporting Countries, Paris: OECD, (1971): 51, (1972): 25, (1973): 25, (1974): 25, (1975): 24, (1976): 24, (1977): 24, (1978): 24.

long road of Sino-American understanding."[20] American enthusiasm during the Vietnam War eventually cooled down; in fact the huge human and economic loss in the Vietnam war provoked outrage. In terms of the death toll, more than 46,000 American soldiers died during the conflict.[21] In addition, in 1970, more bombs had been dropped in Vietnam than at any other time in history.[22] The withdrawal of American troops from Vietnam, elaborated further by Fairbank, would be "accompanied by an effort to normalize relations with China."[23]

Henry Kissinger had revealed the decision to withdraw troops from Vietnam in his memoirs White House Years. In the memorandum that he sent to the President on 10 September 1969, he explained that "I do not believe that with our current plans we can win the war within two years, although our success or failure in hurting the enemy remains very important."[24] The problem was to decide in which way and by which means the withdrawal could be facilitated without affecting the long-term interests of the United States as well as preventing further penetration of the Soviet influence in Vietnam. The eventual withdrawal was put forward by the Eight Points that Kissinger prepared with General Vernon A. Walters. The Eight Points dealt with procedural matters such as the time and the process as well as conceptual matters such as support for the reunification of Vietnam.[25]

Here, in light of diplomatic relations, the Vietnam War, certainly, helped to explain some of the imperatives that the United States needed to reconcile, perhaps not by its own effort but by the facilitation of the world economy. However, the rapprochement with China was also denied by Kissinger as a "Card" to be played with the former Soviet Union. Instead, he mentioned that the facilitation of the visit was based on a "common concern."

> Equilibrium was the name of the game. We did not seek to join China in a provocative confrontation with the Soviet Union. But we agreed on the necessity to curb Moscow's geopolitical ambitions. The sending of combat troops to Egypt, the circumstances that led to the Syrian invasion of Jordan, the building of a naval base at Cienfuegos, and the clashes along the Sino-Soviet border were part of a uniform challenge to the global equilibrium that had to be resisted. Moreover, both China and the United States wanted to broaden their diplomatic options: Peking, to escape the self-imposed isolation of the Cultural Revolution; Washington, to strengthen security in an international system less dependent for stability on permanent American intervention.[26]

The amelioration of U.S. unilateral influence would, therefore, suggest the search for an alternative reason underlying their relations. As mentioned earlier, the dollars crisis in 1971 juxtaposed the urgent U.S. search for a remedy to the crisis against the need to sustaining its hegemonic power. Political commentary that appeared in *Time* magazine on 30 August 1971, hinted at the reason for Nixon's visit to China was denoted, "What he did in foreign policy with his approach to Peking he outdid in domestic affairs last week.... The claim was merited. A show of firm leadership was clearly needed in order to get the U.S. industrial machine running smoothly once more."[27] Immediately after the announcement of the devaluation of the U.S. dollar, Nixon swiftly launched his "package" of economic policy at home. The program included the reduction of government spending by 4.7 billion, a 10 percent industrial credit and 10 percent import surcharge.[28]

In terms of artificial devaluation, some statesmen and financiers perceived such a "reluctant" move "as an unthinkable national humiliation and a devastating blow to the non-Communist world's financial system, which uses the dollar as the central trading currency."[29] Susan Strange described the U.S. dollar as "top currency", defining it as "the currency of the state that has world economic leadership, the currency of the predominant state in the international economy."[30] Apparently, these statesman and financiers did not understand that the artificial devaluation was not because the United States had succumbed to any one system but because of the natural prevailing forces of market liberalism. To reconcile such domestic resentments with the international community, Nixon attempted to take the initiative in preparing for the trip to China. In terms of foreign policy initiatives, that presentation and trip earned him kudos for his boldness and proved that Nixon could initiate the reorientation of foreign policy. In reality, as concurred by Roy Bennett, senior research associate at the Center for Policy Research, it was about time "there would be a reciprocal benefit in opening the world's market to vast United States exports and investments."[31]

The Preparations

In 1967, Nixon had exhibited his willingness to pave the way for rapprochement with China. His *blueprint* or the so-called *guideline for operation* was first introduced in the October 1967 issue of *Foreign Affairs*. The framework of his rapprochement with China was anchored in his belief "that communism is not necessarily the wave of Asia's future."[32] However, when he examined the growth of South Korea, Thailand, Japan, Hong Kong and Taiwan, he concluded that "a prime reliance on private enterprise and on the pricing mechanism of the market as the chief determinant of business decision;..."[33] In other words, it appeared that normalization with China was an extension of his objectives to influence and change China.[34] Therefore, preparations before the final trip were organized with a sophisticated craftsmanship.

The "leak" of his intention to normalize relations with China was also facilitated by "Yahya channel" and "Romanian channel."[35] Both the president of Pakistan, Yahya Khan and the president of Romania, Nicolae Ceauescu agreed to help as an intermediary to bring those messages of normalization to China. Their efforts yielded results when Chou En-lai, the vice premier of China replied that "If the United States has a desire to settle the issue and a proposal for its solution, the PRC will be prepared to receive a U.S. special envoy in Peking."[36]

In response, instead of playing with words and diplomatic tone, Nixon announced a termination of the trade embargo against China on 14 April 1971, based on market and economic incentive.[37] Subsequently, Nixon had arranged the "procedure" for the groundwork to be laid before his final visit. He mentioned clearly in his memoirs how to formulate the preparation:

> We arranged that Kissinger would fly to Vietnam for consultations early in July and then stop in Pakistan on the way back. There he would develop a stomachache that would require him to stay in bed and not be seen by the press. Then, with President Yahya's cooperation, he would be taken to an airport where a Pakistani jet would fly him over the mountains into China. The stomachache was scheduled for July 9–11. Kissinger would then fly to San Clemente to report to me.[38]

According to Nixon, Kissinger's trip resulted in "Eureka"—codeword that had been agreed upon earlier, before the trip between Nixon and Kissinger, which indicated that the arrangement of the trip to China was a success.[39] When compared to Kissinger's second trip to China on 20 October 1971—a trip to settle the agenda and prepare the substantial details of Nixon's trip[40]—the first trip was truly ground-breaking.

In order to have full confidence in the historic visit, Nixon's last preparations actually included psychological readiness. He invited the French philosopher André Malraux to the White House for the last bit of advice on the analysis of both Mao and himself. Malraux described Mao as "a man inhabited by a vision" and "possessed by it."[41] However, he encouraged Nixon to take the initiative because "You are about to attempt one of the most important things of our century,... What you are going to do, Mr. President, might well have a totally different outcome from whatever is anticipated."[42]

At last, Nixon's trip in February 1972 to China clearly marked a tremendous catharsis in terms of human perspective toward the capitalist and communist camps. It mattered not whether he was "the champion of capitalism"[43] (as *Time* magazine described him), his trip illustrated, even precipitated the true importance of diplomatic relations between two countries, and served to facilitate the establishment of an international political economy.

Notes

1. Bruce Cumings, "The World Shakes China" *The National Interest*, no. 43 (Spring 1996): 29.
2. Jerome Alan Cohen, Robert F. Dernberger and John R. Garson, *China Trade Prospects and U.S. Policy* (New York: Praeger Publishers, 1971).
3. Ibid., 249–265.
4. Ibid., 272.
5. The gold standard system was a product of the Bretton Woods conference held in New Hampshire in 1944. Those countries that participated in the conference agreed to accept the U.S. dollar as the major currency for the international monetary system. In essence, the gold standard functioned on the guarantee of the United States to convert the gold at $35 an once at anytime. Since holding gold by itself does not generate interest, those countries, therefore, demand U.S. dollars. In such circumstance, the heavy demand for U.S. dollars, in the long-run, inevitably, contribute to the breakdown of the U.S. dollar. See Robert S. Walters and David H. Blake, *The Politics of Global Economic Relations*, 4th ed., (Englewood Cliffs, NJ: Prentice-Hall International, Inc., 1992): 73–74. For an in-depth study of the political meaning of the U.S.-dollar crisis, refer to Susan Strange, "The Politics of International Currencies", *World Politics* 23, no. 2 (January 1971): 2115–31 and Susan Strange, "Protectionism and World Politics", *International Organization* 39, no. 2 (Spring 1985): 233–60. See also David P.

Calleo, Harold Van B. Cleveland and Leonard Silk, "The Dollar and the Defense of the West" in *International Political Economy: A Reader*, edited by Kendall W. Stiles and Tsuneo Akaha, (New York: HarperCollins Publishers, 1991): 69–82.

6. *The New York Times Index 1972* (New York: The New York Times Company, 1973): 820.

7. *The New York Times Index 1971* (New York: The New York Times Company, 1972): 781.

8. Michael Pillsbury, "U.S. (Chinese Military Ties?" *Foreign Policy*, no. 20 (Fall 1975): 50–64 and Roger Glenn Brown, "Chinese Politics and American Policy: A New Look at the Triangle" *Foreign Policy*, no. 23 (Summer 1976): 3–23. Obviously, there is an abundance of articles and books on Nixon's visit, nevertheless, these two are distinctive not only because of their unique interpretations but also because of their insightful hypotheses. Moreover, particular articles are described by Lowell Dittmer as "among the best..." See Lowell Dittmer, "The Strategic Triangle: An Elementary Game-Theoretical Analysis" *World Politics* 33, no. 4 (July 1981): 485.

9. Pillsbury, "U.S.-Chinese Military Ties," 50.

10. Ibid., 56.

11. Ibid., 57.

12. Ibid., 57–58.

13. Brown, "Chinese Politics and American Policy: A New Look at the Triangle," 4–8.

14. Ibid., 8–10.

15. John S. Hodgson and Mark G. Herander, *International Economic Relations*, (Englewood Cliffs, NJ: Prentice-Hall International, Inc., 1983): 259 and see also Bo Sodersten, *International Economics*, 2d ed., (London: Macmillan, 1980): 239–242.

16. Joint Economic Committee Congress of the United States, *The Future of U.S. Foreign Trade Policy: Hearings before the Subcommittee on Foreign Economic Policy*, vol. 1, 90th Cong., 1st sess., July 11, 12, 13, 18, 19 and 20, 1967, 4.

17. Ibid., 278.

18. Ibid., 278–279.

19. Richard G. Lipsey, Peter O. Steiner, and Douglas D. Purvis, *Economics*, 7th ed., (New York: Harper and Row, 1984): 231.

20. John King Fairbank, *The United States and China*, 4th ed, Enlarged (Cambridge, MA: Harvard University Press, 1983): 457.

21. Stephen E. Ambrose, *Rise to Globalism: American Foreign Policy Since 1938*, 7th rev. ed., London: Penguin Books, 1993): 251.

22. Ibid., 204.

23. Ibid., 458.

24. Henry Kissinger, *White House Years* (Boston: Little Brown and Company, 1979): 1481.

25. Ibid., 1489–1490.

26. Ibid., 764.

27. *Time* magazine, 30 August 1971, 4.

28. Ibid., 4.

29. *Time* magazine, 27 December 1971, 14.

30. Susan Strange, "The Politics of International Currencies" *World Politics* 23, no. 2 (January 1971): 221.

31. Roy Bennett, "Nixon's New Foreign Policy: The Next Four Years" in *What Nixon's is Doing to Us*, edited by Alan Garter, Colin Greer and Frank Riessman, (New York: Haper and Row, 1973): 251.

32. Richard M. Nixon, "Asia after Vietnam," *Foreign Affairs* 46, no. 1 (Oct. 1967): 111.
33. Ibid., 118–119.
34. Ibid., 121.
35. Richard Nixon, *RN: The Memoirs of Richard Nixon* (London: Sidgwick and Jackson, 1978): 546.
36. Ibid., 547.
37. Ibid., 548.
38. Ibid., 553.
39. Ibid.
40. Ibid., 555.
41. Ibid., 558.
42. Ibid.
43. *Time* magazine, 28 February 1972, 15.

7

A Change of U.S. Power Context and China's Adaptation to the World Economy

*A reform-minded and modernizing China
will continue to advance toward a market-
driven system guided by law rather than by
corrupt families and will better meet the
material needs of its citizens.* [1]
—Kenneth Lieberthal

Introduction

This chapter examines the change in U.S. power in relation to China from that of a unilateral military force to one based upon economic opportunity and market openness. The previous chapter illustrated that Nixon's visit to China in 1972 was an externalization of the market force. The end of the Vietnam War gave America a respite from the tensions of the cold war. When Deng Xiaoping officially regained his membership in the Politburo and was back on the political stage in August 1973,[2] it seemed that China was ripe for change. The Cultural Revolution had damaged the economy and political structure. A political breakthrough was needed. The Open Door Policy adopted in 1978 paved the way for China to enter the world economy.

Of course, joining the global stage carries with it certain concessions and responsibilities. For China to participate in global trading and monetary organizations such as GATT (superseded by the WTO in 1995), the IMF, and the IRBD (later the World Bank)[3] requires give and take.

To gain membership to the WTO, China has tried to adjust to norms of the world economy that have been largely engineered by the United States. In the study of international relations, this concept is very close to the neo-liberal school that holds that a higher level of control and a set of rules will govern some countries' policy, especially in trade regimes.[4]

This chapter, therefore, is divided into three sections. The first section analyzes how the change in the nature of power, from pure military power to economic or knowledge-based power, affected U.S. policy toward China. The second section pinpoints the use of trade regimes as a means of explaining how China is getting involved in the world economy. The final section introduces the concept of engagement, which is the most recent U.S. policy toward China.

The Change in Power Context and U.S. Policy toward China

The late 1970s and early 1980s witnessed a more pluralistic development of foreign policy among nations of different sizes. If a nation tries not to be drawn into the quagmire of contemporary world politics or even attempts to be captured in the existing situation, it has "to obtain a broad measure of consent on general principles—principles that ensure the supremacy of the leading state and dominant social class—and at the same time to offer some prospect of satisfaction to the less powerful."[5] Sino-American relations represented the United States' manipulation of power in a less unilateral military coercion but on broader bases of consensus.

The test of Sino-America relations was taken one step further when Deng Xiaoping visited the United States in early 1979. The visit was a barometer of U.S.-China relations. Both countries benefited because support of normalization of the U.S. economy was strengthened when Deng appeared before Congress.[6] The U.S.-China Technical Accord, for example, was signed in 1984. It functions as "a general expression of intentions" between these two countries in proceeding toward closer relations.[7]

U.S. leadership in the world is changing as the nature of power changes. Unlike Ray Cline, who defines power by its tangible elements,[8] Joseph Nye believes that "power is becoming less fungible, less coercive, and less tangible."[9] In particular, American culture, language, and ideas will help to sustain American power in the next decade.[10] The Chinese government considers some of these elements to be "spiritual pollution."[11] Nevertheless, the influence of spreading particular kinds of power and the ability to create inspiring ideas is more inclined to be American based. These "soft power resources"[12] sustain America's power.

Over time, the definition of power has enlarged. Robert Gilpin contends that "economic dependence establishes a power relationship that is a fundamental feature of the contemporary world economy."[13] To acquire power through economic success is possible, and through economic build-up, industrialization and modernization. Power, therefore, is an acquired status, not an ascribed one.

The remarkable visit of U.S. President Ronald Reagan to China in April 1984 consolidated the two countries' bilateral relations, albeit at the mercy of the Soviet Union's political strife.[14] It was the first presidential trip to China since Nixon's groundbreaking 1972 visit. Reagan's visit resulted in the signing of a Joint Nuclear Pact with Premier Zhao Ziyang. The pact marked a further step toward world peace through nonproliferation and also opened the opportunity for U.S. industry to bid for a U.S.$20 billion contract in nuclear-sector projects.[15]

In addition, China and U.S. foreign relations were governed more by rules, bilateral treaties, and agreements. In connection with China's move toward the world economy, it would be easier for the United States to use international economic agreements to restrain China's pace of development, at least under the consent of the United States. Some of the important treaties are listed below. They represent the narrowing of ideological differences through mutual adjustment.

Issues such as transport, rescue, and fishing rights included in table 7.1 were considered "low politics" during the cold war. Nevertheless, what was important was the mutual acceptance of these treaties by China and the United States. (More details will be explored in chapter 9). Here, I will illustrate a particular case to show how China's involvement in the international trade regime will eventually shape her course of development.

International Trade Regimes and China's Internationalization

The Process

The establishment of GATT was never smooth. The interwar period was enmeshed in heavy protectionism known as the "beggar-thy-neighbor" policy.[16] International trade was noncooperative. As stated by Robert Walters and David Blake, "protection of domestic industry is to be carried out to the greatest extent possible through tariff duties."[17] In terms of willingness and capability, the United States was the sole choice to lead the development of a global trading regime. The State Department explained:

> The only nation capable of taking the initiative in promoting a worldwide movement toward the relaxation of trade barriers is the United States. Because of its relatively great economic strength, its favorable balance of payments position,

TABLE 7.1
Treaties of Mutual Agreements Signed between the United States
and China in the 1980s (selected)

Date	Agreements	Concerns
30 April 1984	Double Taxation	Avoidance of double taxation and the prevention of tax evasion
23 July 1985	Peaceful Uses of Nuclear Energy	Extensive cooperation on the peaceful uses of nuclear energy on the basis of mutual respect for sovereignty
23 July 1985	Fisheries off the United States Coasts	Common concern for the rational management, conservation and achievement of optimum yield of fish stocks off U.S. coasts
14 March 1986	Aviation: Technical Assistance	Promotion and development of technical cooperation in civil aviation
20 January 1987	Maritime Search and Rescue	Ensure the safety of human life and property at sea and facilitate search and rescue (SAR) operations at sea
15 December 1988	Maritime Transport	Recognizing the importance of maritime relations for both countries

Source: Department of State, "Double Taxation: Taxes on Income," 30 April 1984, *Treaties and Other International Acts Series* (TIAS), no. 12065, 2; Department of State, "Atomic Energy: Peaceful Uses of Nuclear Energy," 23 July 1985, *TIAS*, no. 12027, 2; Department of State, "Fisheries off the United States Coasts," 23 July 1985, *TIAS*, no. 12002, 2–3; Department of State, "Aviation: Technical Assistance," 14 March 1986, *TIAS*, no. 12006, 2–4; Department of State, "Maritime Search and Rescue," 20 January 1987, *TIAS*, no. 12013, 2; Department of State, "Maritime Transport," 15 December 1988, *TIAS*, no. 12026, 2.

and the importance of its market to the well-being of the rest of the world, the influence of the United States on world commercial policies far surpasses that of any other nations.[18]

In fact, the United States originally wanted to construct an International Trade Organization (ITO) more encompassing than GATT. The initiative for this first appeared in the Havana Charter,[19] but was blocked by domestic businesses and protectionists. The charter was eventually prevented from gaining full congressional ratification.[20] The United States, along with seven other countries, then orchestrated, albeit on a smaller scale, a conference on the comprehensive agreement on trade issues. The result of the conference became known as GATT.[21] According to Susan Strange, the concept of free trade under GATT was "...set by the United States, reinforced by the wartime bargain struck with Britain."[22]

Originally, China was a founding member of GATT; the Chinese Nationalist government signed the Agreement on 30 October 1947. However, since Communist takeover after 1949 and to the unfulfilling obligation of the Taiwanese government, China withdrew its membership on 6 March 1950.[23] Furthermore, China's close relationship with the former Soviet Union in the 1950s did not help her become a true member of the world economy, nor did China's isolation policy in the 1960s. At the same time, though, U.S. foreign policy's encroachment in Japan and embankment of the Four Little Dragons was transforming their economic structures through market liberalism.

IPE and Chinese Economic Development

The augmentation of the market liberalism which underpinned the facilitation of the U.S. initiative was realized through the practical study of Chinese economic development and the influence of the world economy and the theoretical exploration of Adam Smith's concept of political economy:

> Political economy, considered as a branch of the science of a statesman or legislator, proposes two distinct objects; first, to provide a plentiful revenue or subsistence for the people, or more properly to enable them to provide such a revenue or subsistence for themselves; and secondly, to supply the state or commonwealth with a revenue sufficient for the public services. It proposes to enrich both the people and the sovereign.[24]

In other words, the political economy crafts a balance between the state's prosperity and the well-being of individuals. Political economy on an international scale helps perpetuate prosperity which can be enjoyed by every state. Under these circumstances, relations between China's participation in GATT and the facilitation of U.S. foreign policy will be substantial.

With reference to their book entitled, *China's Participation in the IMF, the World Bank, and GATT: Toward a Global Economic Order*, Harold K. Jacobson and Michel Oksenberg offer an account of the historical development and the internationalization process of China in terms of joining those organizations.[25] They also try to paint a general picture of the world economy by describing the establishment of the organizations after 1945. If we read between the lines, we can discern from the book that the international economic environment and the formulation of these organizations in trade and finance were tremendously affected by the U.S. initiative and endorsement. In other words, the major implication of China's membership in these organizations centered on its perceptions of those organizations and other members' reactions in relation to China's perceived difficulties upon entering the world economy.

According to Jacobsen and Oksenberg, "the ability to absorb China into the world will be substantially shaped by the perceptions and expectations of the Chinese and their trading partners concerning global economic trends and the consequences of Chinese behavior in international affairs."[26] That is, the process of China's entering the world economy is not static but rather a dynamic interaction of complex economic and political relations among different countries. Existing members will be concerned about whether China will abide by the rules governing each member, given that her unstable political development and the intransigence of the privatization of the state-enterprises.[27]

Nevertheless, China's participation in these Keystone International Economic Organizations (KIEOs) was never smooth sailing. Leaning toward the Soviet Union in the 1950s and then toward domestic self-reliance hampered China's economic development and internationalization.[28] The years before 1976 were marked by ideological confrontation, antagonism, and internal political instability.[29] Nonetheless, the People's Bank of China, the Ministry of Finance, and the Ministry of Foreign Affairs in January 1979 collaborated to formally recommend that China join the IMF and IBRD.[30]

Jacobson and Oksenberg define four phases that mark China's incorporation into the KIEOs: (1) "engagement"; (2) "initial participation"; (3) "mutual adjustment"; and (4) "mutual partnership."[31] *Engagement* begins with the generation of interest and the building of contacts in the negotiation process. *Initial participation* refers to the development of concrete, substantial policy-planning, which for China was in the 1980s.[32] It is fair to say that China remains in the mutual adjustment process, which demands close relationships among the members and the monitoring of each country by the others. At this level "the compatibility between the state and the international organization is tested."[33] As time goes by, there are still many imperfections in this process, for instance, delays in project approval by the inefficient bureaucracy, the complexity of the pricing system, and difficulty in collecting data.[34]

Following this theory, the major problem would be the search for a breakthrough in moving from *mutual adjustment* to *mutual partnership*. It takes great courage and a skillful reconciliation of costs and benefits to move forward to closer commitment to the KIEOs. First, the breakthrough would require that China open her market and reduce import barriers. The more open the market, the more privileges will be enjoyed.[35] But, opening her market also poses a threat to the government in terms of challenges from the rest of the world. Moreover, given China's population, trade volume,[36] and its socialist nature, mutual partnership is indeed a big step. Even though the book is optimistic about China's participation in the KIEOs, the writers still conclude, with some skepticism, that "our study suggests the goal is realistic and worthwhile, but the path will be arduous and full of unanticipated twists and turns."[37]

The twists and turns of China's participation in the KIEOs reached a climax in 1994, the year that wrapped up the Uruguay Round talks' 27,000 pages of agreements and prepared for the switch to WTO in 1995. Trying to jump on the WTO bandwagon and appeal to the members, especially the United States, China presented a basket of trade liberalization and tariff reduction policies. This resulted in several negotiations in April, July, and December 1994 in Geneva.[38] China's efforts were rewarded by its signing of the Final Act Embodying the Results of the Uruguay Round of Multilateral Trade Negotiation (Final Act) and the Agreement Establishing the Multilateral Trade Organization (MTO Agreement) in April 1994,[39] allowing it to be accepted as a GATT Contracting Party. But, China's application to join as a founding member of WTO, was rejected because of its lack of market openness and transparency and its regulated tax system.[40] Eventually, eighty-one countries became founding members of the WTO, while fifty countries were placed on the waiting list, including China.[41]

Actually, U.S. intellectuals and policymakers are sanguine about incorporating China into the WTO. Michael H. Armacost, former U.S. Ambassador to Japan, and Lawrence J. Lau, a Stanford University professor, believe that "America stands to benefit from China's admission. U.S. companies operate best in open, non-discriminatory trade, which can be most readily assured if China participates in GATT."[42] That said, China has to further open its market. In 1995, China agreed to a one-year cut in tariffs on 246 classes of imports as a gesture of its sincerity toward the WTO.[43] Yet members are still waiting for the concrete development of market openness and policy deregulation by China.

The WTO's idea of trade liberalization was realized and marked by the first WTO Ministerial Conference held in Singapore from 9–13 December 1996. The choice of Singapore signified its remarkable triumph as a major contributor toward market openness in trade, and marked her success story in joining the brotherhood of market liberalism of the world economy. The conference ended with the agreement to liberalize global trade in the $400 billion-a-year information technology market by the year 2000.[44] In February 1997, a global phone accord was the first priority of the WTO meeting in Geneva. China, however, faced a dilemma. To facilitate a dramatic deregulation and liberalization would certainly appeal to WTO members. Doing so, however, would inevitably jeopardize the state-run industrial sector.[45] Although most of the industrial sectors were never profitable, they were an important symbol of socialism and employed millions of citizens.

All in all, China's participation in and acceptance by the international organizations entails complex decisions by the Chinese government about long-term commitment and structural change of the existing legal and political systems. It also requires painstaking deliberation among the member countries. Yet, as argued by Renato Ruggiero, Director-General of the WTO, the breakthrough from the Uruguay Round to the establishment of the WTO was a correct move because the countries that joined the WTO are "a referendum of unquestionable support for a system instrumental to growth and development."[46] In a study carried cut by the staff reporters of the *Far Eastern Economic Review*, Beijing's entry into the WTO represented the nurturing effect and perpetuation of market liberalization through trading regimes. They concluded that "China's entry into the WTO will not require that the country immediately conform to world trading norms. It should, however, set clear timetables for China to, say, crack open markets for automobiles, or allow foreign companies to stack their products in their own warehouses."[47] Given China's development process, market force becomes a point of intersection in U.S.-China foreign relations. In addition, in terms of Sino-America cooperation, Zbigniew Brzezinski and Michel Oksenberg even suggested that the United States and China should work together in aspects related to geopolitical relations, the Asian-Pacific region's stability, and democratization.[48]

Engagement and Enlargement

President Clinton's policy toward China was affected by his "baby-boomer" outlook and his intention to drop the cold war containment strategy in favor of a new objective. According to Douglas Brinkley, the search for a catch-phrase for his foreign policy became a central issue during his first months in the Oval Office.[49] After a debate among the National Security Council's (NSC) staff, they eventually came up with the "enlargement" proposal by Jeremy Rosner, the NSC's counselor and senior director for legislative affairs. Anthony Lake, the national security adviser, proclaimed that this proposal served four objectives of America's foreign policy in the post-cold war era. They are:

1. to "strengthen the community of market democracies";
2. to "foster and consolidate new democracies and market economies where possible";
3. to "counter the aggression and support the liberalization of states hostile to democracy"; and
4. to "help democracy and market economies take root in regions of greatest humanitarian concern."[50]

While enlargement has been adopted as the general U.S. foreign policy objective, additionally, the empirical application of such a concept to policy with China can be qualified by "comprehensive engagement."[51] *Comprehensive engagement* was mentioned by Winston Lord, U.S. assistant secretary of state for Asian and Pacific Affairs, during a hearing of the congressional Subcommittee on East Asian and Pacific Affairs on 4 May 1994.[52] According to Winston Lord, assistant secretary of state for East Asian and Pacific Affairs, comprehensive engagement toward China has two levels: "First, it has enabled us to promote our multiple goals with China much more effectively. Second, it has provided a broader framework within which the Chinese leaders have greater latitude and incentive to make progress on human rights issues."[53] U.S. China policy served as a guiding principle to facilitate China's involvement in world activities as well as prompting China to "abide by accepted international norms."[54]

As China pushes to get into the WTO, its participation in other international organizations is not to be neglected. According to the *Yearbook of International Organizations 1996–97*, China is a member of more than 1,848 international governmental and nongovernmental organizations.[55] While Taiwan, according to the same yearbook, only became a member of 1,248 such kinds of organizations.[56] As explained earlier by Stephen D. Krasner, such bodies of "implicit or explicit principles, norms, rules, and decision-making procedures"[57] of these international organizations will collectively transform China in the long run.

The details of how international society serves as a monitoring and transformative force will be discussed in chapter 8. During China's

TABLE 7.2
China's Participation in International Governmental and
Nongovernmental Organizations (selected)*

Asia-Pacific Economic Cooperation (APEC)

Asia-Pacific Telecommunity (APT)

Asian and Pacific Skill Development Program (APSDEP)

Asian Development Bank (ADB)

Asian Regional Term for Employment Promotion (ARTEP)

Asian-Pacific Postal Training Center (APPTC)

International Center for Theoretical Physics (ICTP)

International Commission for Scientific Exploration of the Mediterranean Sea (ICSEM)

International Criminal Police Organization–Interpol (ICPO–Interpol)

International Geological Correlation Program (IGCP)

International Institute of Refrigeration (IIR)

International Maritime Organization (IMO)

Regional Energy Development Program (REDP)

Regional Network for the Chemistry of Natural Products in Southeast Asia

United Nations Fund for Drug Abuse Control (UNFDAC)

United Nations High Commissioner for Refugees (UNHCR)

World Meteorological Organization (WMO)

* Organizations of which Hong Kong is also a member.

Source: Union of International Associations, ed., *Yearbook of International Organizations*, vol. 2, *1996/97* (Munchen: K. G. Saur, 1996): 626–636 and 281–293.

move toward the WTO, the forfeiture of some domestic policies was a preliminary requirement for being accepted by the WTO.

According to Ralph C. Bryant, a senior fellow in the Economic Studies Program at the Brookings Institution, the mutual recognition and active coordination in such economic organizations will, in the intermediate or long run, engender "multilateral surveillance."[58] The comprehensive engagement of U.S. foreign policy will help prepare that kind of transformation.

Notes

1. Kenneth Lieberthal, "A New China Strategy" *Foreign Affairs* 74, no. 6 (November/December 1995): 36.
2. Deng's path to regain power was relatively rapid. In 1975, he was the director of the General Staff Department of the PLA. From January to November 1975,

Deng was the acting premier. Until his formal resignation from the Politbureau of the Chinese Communist Party, the Central Committee and the Standing Committee of the Bureau, and the Central Advisory Commission, he was China's *de facto* paramount leader. See Peter N. S. Lee, *Industrial Management and Economic Reform in China 1949–1984* (Hong Kong: Oxford University Press, 1987): 126 and *Qiushi* 22, no. 13 (1989): 7.

3. Harold K. Jacobson and Michel Oksenberg categorised these organizations as keystone international economic organization (KIEOs). China joined the IMF and World Bank in 1980, and began to apply for full membership in GATT in 1986. See Harold K. Jacobson and Michel Oksenberg, *China's Participation in the IMF, the World Bank, and GATT: Toward a Global Economic Order* (Ann Arbor, MI: University of Michigan Press, 1990): vi. More recent references to the issue of China and the world include Nicholas R. Lardy, *China in the World Economy* (Washington, DC: Institute for International Economics, 1994); Vincent Cable and Peter Ferdinand, "China as an Economic Giant: Threat or Opportunity?" in *International Affairs* 70, no. 2 (1994): 243–261; and Morio Matsumoto, "China's Industrial Policy and Participation in the GATT" in Japan External Trade Organization, *China Newsletter No. 112*, September-October (1994): 2–20. After a series of talks among China, the United States and the member countries, China was not admitted to the WTO. This is said to be a temporary setback in the ongoing process of internationalization. More talks and progress are expected.

4. Jock A. Finlayson and Mark W. Zacher, "The GATT and the Regulation of Trade Barriers: Regime Dynamics and Functions" in *International Regimes*, edited by Stephen D. Krasner (Ithaca, NY: Cornell University Press): 273–314.

5. Joseph S. Nye, Jr., *Bound To Lead: The Changing Nature of American Power* (New York: Basic Books, 1991): 32.

6. *Hong Kong Standard*, 12 January 1979.

7. *South China Morning Post*, 4 January 1984.

8. Ray Cline divides power into two components, tangible and intangible. The formula is:

    $$Pp= (C+E+M) * (S+W), \text{ where:}$$
    Pp= perceived power
    C = critical mass = population + territory
    E = economic capability
    M = military capability
    S = strategic purpose
    W = will to pursue national strategy

    Accordingly, C, E and M are tangible, while S and W are intangible. See Ray S. Cline, *World Power Assessment: A Calculus of Strategic Drift* (Boulder, CO: Westview Press, 1977): 11.

9. Joseph S. Nye, *Bound to Lead*, 188.

10. Ibid., 194–197.

11. Lowell Dittmer, *China Under Reform* (Boulder, CO: Westview Press, 1994): 129

12. Joseph S. Nye, *Bound to Lead*, 200.

13. Robert Gilpin, *The Political Economy of International Relations* (Princeeton, NJ: Princeton University Press, 1987): 10.

14. *South China Morning Post*, 27 April 1984.

15. *South China Morning Post*, 28 April 1984.

16. Robert S. Walters and David H. Blake, *The Politics of Global Economic Relations*, 4th ed. (Englewood Cliffs, NJ: Prentice-Hall International, Inc., 1992): 14.

17. Ibid.
18. Joan Edelman Spero, *The Politics of International Economic Relations*, 4th ed. (London: Routledge, 1992): 68.
19. The Havana Charter "was an essential part of the plan to create a new, internationally managed economic system in the postwar era and, like the rest of that plan, was a product of strong U.S. leadership." See Joan Edelman Spero, *The Politics of International Economic Relations*, 4th ed. (London: Routledge, 1992): 68.
20. Ibid., 69.
21. John S. Hodgson and Mark G. Herander, *International Economic Relations* (Englewood Cliffs, NJ: Prentice-Hall, Inc., 1983): 256.
22. Susan Strange, *States and Markets*, 2d ed. (London: Pinter Publisher, 1994): 186.
23. Wenguo Cai, "China's GATT Membership: Selected Legal and Political Issues" *Journal of World Trade* 26, no. 1 (February 1992): 36.
24. Adam Smith, *An Inquiry into the Nature and Causes of the Wealth of Nations*, vol. 1, eds. R. H. Campbell and A. S. Skinner (Oxford: Clarendon Press, 1976): 428.
25. Harold K. Jacobson and Michel Oksenberg, *China's Participation in the IMF, the World Bank, and GATT: Toward a Global Economic Order* (Ann Arbor, MI: The University of Michigan Press, 1990).
26. Ibid., 13.
27. Ibid., 160–162.
28. During the 1950s and 1960s, the analysis of Chinese foreign relations was dominated by the theory of the "strategic triangle." See John W. Garver, *Foreign Relations of the People's Republic of China* (Englewood Cliffs, NJ: Prentice-Hall, 1993).
29. Although greatly criticized, the article most cited with reference to factionalism in CCP was Andrew J. Nathan, "A Factionalism Model for CCP Politics" in *China Quarterly*, no. 53 (Jan./Mar., 1973): 34–66. There are many books referring to the disturbing years, such as Roderick MacFarquhar and John K. Fairbank, eds., *The Cambridge History of China, volume 14, The People's Republic, part 1: The Emergence of Revolutionary China, 1949–1965* (London: Cambridge University Press, 1987) and Kuang Sheng Liao, *Antiforeignism and Modernization in China*, 3d ed. (Hong Kong: The Chinese University Press, 1990): chapter 10.
30. Harold K. Jacobson and Michel Oksenberg, *China's Participation*, 69.
31. Ibid., 107.
32. Ibid., 107–128.
33. Ibid., 107.
34. Ibid., 152–154.
35. Ibid., 158.
36. The trade volume between China and ASEAN in the first half of 1994 was $5.518 billion dollars, 43.1 percent more than that of the previous year. The United States trade deficit with China was well over $29.5 billion dollars in 1994. Sources from *China Daily*, 9–15 October 1994 and the *International Herald Tribune*, 18–19 February 1995, 9, respectively.
37. Harold K. Jacobson and Michel Oksenberg, *China's Participation*, 169.
38. *Hong Kong Economic Journal*, 11 April 1994, 7; *Hong Kong Economic Journal*, 12 July 1994, 6; *International Herald Tribune*, 25 July 1994, 7 and *Hong Kong Economic Journal*, 22 December 1997, 2.
39. Guiguo Wang, "China's Return to GATT: Legal and economic Implications" *Journal of World Trade* 28, no. 3 (June 1994): 51.

40. Ibid.
41. *South China Morning Post*, 15 July 1995, 1.
42. *International Herald Tribune*, 20 December 1994, 4.
43. *International Herald Tribune*, 18 January 1995.
44. *Hong Kong Economic Journal*, 14 December 1996, 2.
45. *International Herald Tribune*, 13 February 1997, 1 and 7.
46. *International Herald Tribune*, 27 December 1996, 8.
47. Matt Forney and Nigel Holloway, "In Two Minds," *Far Eastern Economic Review*, 19 June 1997, 68–69.
48. Zbigniew Brzezinski and Michel Oksenberg, "If China and America Learn to Work Together," *International Herald Tribune*, 17 June 1997, 8.
49. Douglas Brinkley, "Democratic Enlargement: The Clinton Doctrine", *Foreign Policy*, no. 106 (Spring 1997): 113.
50. Ibid., 116.
51. Joseph S. Nye, Jr., "The Case for Deep Engagement," *Foreign Affairs* 74, no. 4 (July/August 1995): 94.
52. U.S. Senate Committee on Foreign Relations, *U.S. Policy toward China: Hearing before the Subcommittee on East Asian and Pacific Affairs*, 103d Cong., 2d sess., 4 May 1994, 4.
53. Ibid.
54. Ibid.
55. Union of International Associations, ed., *Yearbook of International Organizations*, vol. 2: *1996–97* (Munchen: K. G. Saur, 1996): 281–293.
56. Ibid., 1392–1400.
57. Stephen D. Krasner, "Structural Causes and Regime Consequences: Regimes as Intervening Variables," in *International Regimes*, edited by Stephen D. Krasner (Ithaca, NY: Cornell University Press, 1983): 2.
58. Ralph C. Bryan, *International Coordination of National Stabilization Policies* (Washington, DC: The Brookings Institution, 1995): 114.

Part Four

U.S. Engagement with China

8

U.S. Foreign Policy Divergences with China

Despite current tensions, China and the United
States continue, in my view, to have a common
interest in shaping the peaceful evolution of Asia.[1]
—Henry A. Kissinger

Introduction

In this chapter I will explore some important discrepancies between China and the United States in the course of the construction of their foreign policy after the cold war. The crackdown on 4 June 1989 of the student demonstration witnessed a historical moment when the illusion of government reform and hope was shattered by the internal politics of China. However, some scholars considered the event as an inescapable period for the development of civil society.[2] In terms of Sino-American foreign relations, nevertheless, the incident was considered to be a new phase in their foreign relations. Right after the incident, the U.S. House of Representatives and Senate attempted to adopt an abortive resolution to impose sanctions on China between 29 June and 4 July 1989.[3] Despite the various comments, severe criticisms from the U.S. government and even the curb on loans, Sino-American trade was not affected. A U.S. $10.4 billion of Balance of Payment Deficit was recorded in 1990.[4]

The dilemma between the economic and political balance of U.S. policy toward China is considered a foreign policy divergence between them. Among others, intellectual property rights, the Taiwan issue and facilitation of the MFN status as a tool to monitor China's progress in human rights are the most encompassing bones of contention. The following sections are devoted to the analysis of these factors which will affect future Sino-America relations.

Intellectual Property Rights (IPR) Disputes

The trigger of possible trade sanctions between the United States and China was released when both sides finally reached an agreement over the trade disputes regarding piracy and property rights on 17 June 1996. Accordingly, China agreed to close down fifteen factories which were named by the United States as producers of pirated compact discs. Moreover, China also accepted the opening of its market to American goods, especially film and media products.[5] In the short run, the agreement between U.S. trade representative Charlene Barshefsky and Chinese representative Zhang Yuejiao eased problems in property rights and piracy. However, the political brinkmanship between the two countries has not guaranteed successful long-run economic and foreign relations. If a settlement had not been reached, the implementation of trade sanctions on Chinese imports would have been a serious setback to both sides' engagement policy, a result which was mutually unwanted. In retrospect, Sino-American relations have been at a nadir since China launched military exercises near Taiwanese soil before Taiwan's presidential election in March 1996. What both sides need, in the long run, is a solution which can realize their wants without degenerating further their "fragile relations."[6]

Historical Development, Process, and the
Immediate Results of Disputes in IPR

China adopted an economic open door policy after the Third Plenum of the CCP's Eleventh Central Committee in December 1978. Since then, trade, economic openness, modernization, and marketization have become the major developmental goals. Trade relations with many developing as well as developed countries have constituted a gigantic component of its economic activities during this process. In general, China's economic development has been unprecedented. In addition, as William Overholt demonstrates in his book *The Rise of China*, China's trade relations with the United States have leaned more toward closeness and cooperation than antagonism and hostility.[7] Moreover, Zbigniew Brzezinski, former security advisor to U.S. President Jimmy Carter, recently called for an open invitation for China to join the Group of Seven because "China is a genuine economic success and a major military power."[8]

However, in reality, trade relations between China and the United States have had twists and turns. Bilateral trade between China and the

TABLE 8.1
U.S. Trade Imbalance with China (1988–1996) (in U.S. $1 billion)

Year	U.S. exports	U.S. Imports	U.S. Balance
1988	5.0	8.5	–3.5
1989	5.8	12.0	–6.2
1990	4.8	15.2	–10.4
1991	6.2	19.0	–12.8
1992	7.5	25.7	–18.3
1993	8.8	31.5	–22.8
1994	9.3	38.8	–29.5
1995	11.7	45.6	–33.9
1996*	12.0	51.5	–39.5

* Data from *Beijing Review*, 7–13 April 1997, 21.
Source: *The China Business Review* 23, no. 3 (May–June 1996): 41.

United States has enhanced China's economic development, but at the same time trade frictions such as balance of payment deficits, infringement on IPR and environmental degradation have emerged. Undeniably, the vigorous trade between China and the United States has benefited the former more than the latter. For example, from 1985 to 1993, U.S. imports from China increased by 716 percent; while, U.S. exports to China increased 128 percent.[9] In addition, the U.S. trade deficit with China hit a record from 1988 to 1996.

The cumulative effects of this deficit have inevitably placed pressure on the U.S. government to further trade agreements and negotiations. Benefiting from the MFN treatment which has been granted by all trading partners in 1980[10] as well as the heavy demand for Chinese goods, China's trade with the United States has become more important, not only in monetary terms but also in terms of the fairness and openness of trading practices.

According to Article 5 of the Memorandum of Understanding between the Government of the United States and the PRC on the Protection of Intellectual Property, "Both Governments will provide procedures and remedies to prevent or stop, internally and at their borders, infringement of intellectual property rights and to deter further infringement."[11] Under these circumstances, China and the United States have mutually agreed to respect and observe the rules and binding forces underpinning their trade relations. Moreover, China also agreed to accede to the Berne Convention for the Protection of Literary and Artistic

Works and the Convention for the Protection of Producers of Phonograms against Unauthorized Duplication of Their Phonograms.[12] As a signing party, China's commitment and the enforcement of IPR protection has thus become a substantial issue.

The Process and Escalation of Confrontation

According to a recent report prepared by the United States General Accounting Office (GAO) entitled *U.S.-China Trade: Implementation of Agreements on Market Access and Intellectual Property*, the Chinese government was considered to have made some progress in strengthening the laws and regulations of IPR protection, but remained weak in their enforcement and implementation.[13] In recent years, the United States has presented several options to the Chinese government to improve IPR protection: maintaining bilateral discussions, listing China under the "Super 301" clause and cooperating with other international organizations such as the World Intellectual Property Organization (WIPO) and GATT/WTO to provide the Chinese government with education and training.[14]

Nevertheless, these measures have contributed very little to preventing IPR infringement in China. In the first place, IPR laws apply differently to the central and provincial governments.[15] For example, administration for industry and commerce on the provincial level is theoretically under the jurisdiction of the State Administration for Industry and Commerce at the state level. The former has the right to review and decide on trademark infringement issues as well as the right to "enforce the local trademark regulations, which may be different from those of the central government or another province's regulations."[16] The uneven distribution of power has given rise to confusion and sluggishness in processing infringement complaints. Secondly, enforcement rights and the responsibilities of different ministries are loosely defined.[17] For instance, the Press and Publications Administration, the Ministry of Radio and Television, and the Ministry of Culture respond individually under different circumstances, but there are no clear boundaries for the proper management of complaints.[18] Last but not least, each individual ministry has a unique jurisdiction over which foreign sound recording should be imported to China. Accordingly, sixty-seven audio-visual companies are under the control of the Ministry of Radio and Television while twenty companies are monitored by the Ministry of Culture.[19] That kind of responsibility-sharing system generates the basic problem of conflict of interest since the more companies under one's jurisdiction, the higher the possibility of being accused of infringement. As long as no one wants to be charged with infringement, it is only natural to complicate matters and create more loopholes before filing the complaints.

As a result, IPR problems have escalated. The first case involving a complaint over IPR infringement on software by the Business Software Alliance (BSA) was filed with the Intellectual Property Tribunal of the Beijing Intermediate People's Court in March 1994.[20] Five Chinese retail stores were charged with selling unauthorized software. Eventually, Chinese officials "seized more than three hundred software programs, CD-ROM disks, and six computers suspected of containing illegal software."[21] At about the same period, on 17 March 1994, the Microsoft Corporation of the United States won a similar case and was compensated 48,693.46 *yuan* after a verdict by the Shenzhen Municipal Industry and Commerce Administration Bureau.[22] The verdict ended a two-and-a-half-year case in which Microsoft accused the Reflective Material Factory of Shenzhen University of producing the unique hologram "MICROSOFT" and "MS-DOS" labels that were widely found in much of the counterfeit software.[23] However, the modicum compensation did not cover the true losses which resulted from the infringement. Cases such as this have not been haphazard individual cases; they have revealed a growing problem for the United States—heavier trade with China will heighten the possibility of IPR infringement by retail outlets.

The Immediate Cause and Consequences

On 26 February 1995, China and the United States signed the PRC–U.S. Intellectual Property Rights Protection Understanding. According to this understanding, China has to begin efforts to enforce IPR by initiating short-term as well as long-term programs. In the short-run, China was expected to launch intensive investigations against any manufacturers that produced pirated products. In the long-run, more cooperative actions between state and municipal levels were expected to be taken in order to enforce IPR.[24] However, China could not live up to the commitments it made in the Agreements and the United States thus condemned China for not doing its utmost to implement said requirements. As a result, factors which infringed on IPR blossomed, greatly damaging the interests of American businesses, especially in the areas of music, films, and software products. For instance, it is believed that there are more than thirty factories producing 100 million pirated compact disks and CD-ROMs in Guangdong province.[25] The United States, having no alternative, threatened to impose a U.S.$2 billion sanction on imports from China if no substantial measures to combat piracy were taken before the deadline of 17 June 1996. In retaliation and in the name of "safeguarding state sovereignty and national dignity",[26] the Chinese also threatened to impose similar sanctions, effective the same day, on U.S. imports if sanctions were imposed, *de facto*, on China. Eventually, the threatened sanctions were dropped after an agreement was reached between China and the United States in which China agreed to close down fifteen factories and allow U.S. imports of cultural and media products. Thus, the latest figures indicated that the pace of anti-piracy policy gained momentum. However, as Chen Jiakui, Head of Guangdong's office on copyright violations, mentioned "...that winning the fight against piracy would involve far more than arresting the factory managers and that backers (often Hong Kong and Taiwan businessmen involved in organized crime)—are more difficult to catch."[27] Future intellectual property rights disputes between China and the U.S. will be their bones of contention.

Taiwan as Intervening Variable

Taiwan and the U.S. Enlargement of Relationship

According to Winston Lord, the formal position of the United States on Taiwanese issues will be "friendly but unofficial."[28] In terms of relations toward China, engagement and enlargement are the principal factors, conveyed by Joseph S. Nye, Jr., the former assistant secretary of defense for international security affairs.[29] Nevertheless, the relations between the U.S. and Taiwan are still captured in the Taiwan Relations Act and the three Joint Communiqués.[30]

The 104th Congress passed a bill on 6 April 1995. The added section 19 clearly declared that "there are no legitimate foreign policy grounds for preventing members of the government chosen by the people of Taiwan from making private visits to the United States."[31] The new amendment allows elected leaders or representatives of the Republic of China (ROC) to pay a visit to the United States.[32] The most significant political achievement of Taiwan in the recent decades came when President Lee Teng-hui of Taiwan was elected in March 1996. Appar-

TABLE 8.2
Chronological Developments of Taiwan's Activities Deemed
Provocative by Mainland China (selected)

Date	Events
August 1996	Lien Chan's stopover in the United States
August 1996	Taiwan's government delayed the approval of investment to China
December 1996	Taiwan curbs trade with China as retaliation to South Africa's rapprochement to Mainland China
December 1996	Meetings on National Development
January 1997	Dalai Lama accepts invitation to Taiwan

Source: *International Herald Tribune*, 8 August 1996, 5; 17–18 August 1996, 1; 30 November–1 December 1996, 5; 14 January 1997, 4 and *China Times* 26 December 1996, 2.

ently, President Lee's visit to Cornell University was based on this amendment. The governments of the United States and Taiwan orchestrated the grand tour.

In terms of domestic politics, the election was a political triumph. However, in terms of Sino-American relations, it nearly became the immediate cause of the entire breakdown in their foreign relations. A series of military exercises came afterward. The uncompromising and drastic missile tests and military exercises before and after the election in the north of Taiwan (a hairbreadth away from the coastal area on a world map scale) clearly portrayed the Chinese government's wrath with Taiwan's newly elected president, Lee Teng-hui, as well as his visit to his alma mater, Cornell University.[33]

In fact, Taiwan's general election consolidated its pace of internationalization. Its strive for international recognition was followed by the policy of *global reach*. Uneasy with the enormous economic success while making little progress in international political development, Prime Minister Lien Chan took the opportunity to travel abroad after Lee's visit to Cornell. No sooner had he finished a quick trip to the Dominican Republic in August 1996, as an honorable guest at the presidential inauguration, than he turned up in Kiev, Ukraine in a ceremony to receive an honorary degree. Both activities were deemed outrageous by the Chinese government. The above activities in table 8.2 are among those practiced by Taiwan in order to provoke China.

Politically, the government of Taiwan is playing a game of seesaw in manipulating money and power. Strong economic growth bolsters

Taiwan's economic health, but since her international political power is still encapsulated by the Chinese military threat, Taiwan has to build its international recognition in other ways: a trip to American alma mater, a seat at the presidential inauguration, acceptance of an honorary degree, and so forth. Nevertheless, whether economic power can be translated into political muscle also depends on its U.S. relations, either governed in the Taiwan Relations Act or facilitated by further U.S. foreign policy. Understandably, stability in the Asian-Pacific region is still a fundamental national interest of the United States.

Taiwan and China's Complex Relations

To begin with, the relationship between Taiwan and China is complicated as well as controversial. It is complicated because their relations are characterized by interwoven, mixed feelings of long cultural bondage and realistic antagonism. In retrospect, the bombardment of the island of Taiwan and the Taiwan Straits incident in the late 1950s laid the underlying threat of military attack from Communist China. Still worse, Taiwan lost her seat in the United Nations in the fall of 1971. That incident, nevertheless, motivated Taiwan to restore its international status in other areas or through other regional organizations. Internally, Taiwan is running her own government under a democratic system. The presidential election was held in 1996. Acknowledging those economic developments (as discussed in chapter three) and democratization, the future road that leads to "peaceful unification" depends on Taiwan and China's genuine and sincere talks, which should take a long time, nevertheless. If Taiwan's Straits Exchange Foundation (SEF) and the Association for Relations across the Taiwan Straits (ARATS) of China can quickly resume contact[34] with each other, the gap between them will be bridged more easily.

On the contrary, if we look at their economic relationship in recent years, the picture is more promising, or even astonishing. Throughout the years, economic and trade relations between Taiwan and mainland China were on the increase, especially when China launched its Open Door Policy in 1979. It can be seen from table 8.3 that bilateral trade between Taiwan and China has been growing gradually.

Moreover, Taiwan's huge foreign exchange has been channeled to the Mainland. Up to 1995, more than 15 billion dollars have been invested in China.[35] It can be seen from the evidence available that Taiwan and China have been conducting a colossal trade and economic

TABLE 8.3

Trade Dependency Ratio between Taiwan and China (1979–1994)

Unit: percent

Year	Taiwan with China		
	Export	Import	Total
1979	0.13	0.38	0.25
1980	1.19	0.39	0.79
1981	1.7	0.35	1.05
1982	0.88	0.44	0.68
1983	0.63	0.44	0.55
1984	1.4	0.58	1.06
1985	2.04	0.58	2.17
1986	2.29	0.60	1.49
1987	3.7	0.83	1.38
1988	4.38	1.22	2.47
1989	4.38	1.22	2.94
1990	4.88	1.4	3.32
1991	6.12	1.79	4.16
1992	7.72	1.55	4.83
1993	9.25	1.43	5.36
1994*	15.17	1.39	8.3

*January–April

Source: *Hong Kong and Macau Monthly* (in Chinese), ROC Executive Yuan China Committee, 15 July 1994, 28.

relationship. Subsequently, a more subtle argument behind the increase of investment in the Mainland, nevertheless, could be problematic particularly when their political and foreign relationships were in trouble. The suspicion is, undoubtedly, the most fundamental concern of the Taiwanese. It follows the debate of whether this kind of investment should be limited to an extent that it can be controlled within the hands of the Taiwan government.

At last, it is not a simple investment opportunity once the door of the Mainland has been opened. The calculation includes the economic benefit of different investors, the foreign policy initiations of Taiwan, the repercussion effect of the Mainland and the perception of the United States. It is, *de facto*, a crucial matter to which we should pay very close attention in order to see what happens in the future. If economic measures become the dominant orientation of foreign policy, one should also weigh the risk of putting nearly all one's eggs in a single basket, which in terms of political sensitivity, is a very risky activity.

MFN as Monitoring Tool

In general, the most-favored-nation status has long been used as the tool to monitor communist countries' economic activators in the world economy. In 1951, The Trade Agreements Suspension Act of the U.S. prohibited the MFN status to Former Soviet Union and China.[36] In 1974, the Act was amended under the Jackson-Vanik amendment. The amendment allowed the United States to provide MFN status to nonmarket economies on the condition that the U.S. president should report twice a year to the Congress if those nonmarket economies impede their emigration policy.[37]

In particular, China was awarded MFN status in 1980 under the U.S.-China Trade Agreement as a result of the 1979 formal normalization agreement. Sino-American economic and business relations suddenly burst into an all-round cooperation. According to a congressional hearing held in 1982, for example, in 1981, Chinese representatives from the Shanghai Investment and Trust Corporation (SITCO) visited the U.S. Department of Commerce and the Chinese representatives of the International Trade Research Institute of the Ministry of Foreign Trade paid a visit to the United States to study market research techniques.[38] In essence, the award of MFN status to those nonmarket economies was justified by the national interests of the United States. The hearing remarked:

> MFN status for Hungary, Romania, and China have served U.S. economic interests well and should continue to do so in the future. Extension of the waiver authority under Section 402 of the Trade Act for these countries is in our national interest. It will continue the development of our economic and commercial relations with these countries and support the expansion of our economic cooperation on a firm and enduring basis.[39]

Seeing the improvement of Sino-American economic relations, the foreign policy orientation was disrupted by the Chinese crackdown on the student demonstration in Tiananmen Square. Used as the monitoring tool, argued Nicholas R. Lardy, the MFN toward China was thereafter used "as a major lever to encourage the Chinese government to improve human rights, to limit the spread of nuclear weapons and to further open China's market to U.S. goods in order to reduce the large and growing bilateral trade imbalance."[40]

On both 29 May and 26 June 1991, a special hearing was organized by the Committee of Foreign Affairs on the issue of MFN status for China.[41] Among others, the participants included Winston Lord, Former American ambassador to China, Richard Holbrooke, assistant secretary of state for East Asia, Edward Friedman, professor of political science at the University of Wisconsin, Fang Lizhi, a leading Chinese advocate for democracy and Zhao Haiqing, a representative from the International Federation of Chinese Students in the United States.[42]

Commercial as well as political policy, the MFN status with China, however, was strongly characterized by the facilitation of its influence to China to abide by the international rules. As proclaimed during the hearing, MFN was vital because "If we deny MFN to the PRC, it's argued, China will happily withdraw into its cocoon and we will hurt progressive elements in the ruling elite in addition to losing all of our influence with that nation."[43] Clearly, MFN as "a key instrument of leverage with China"[44] was embodied in the general framework of this policy.

In addition to intellectual property rights infringement and market openness, the facilitation of MFN as an instrument to induce China to recognize universal human rights was further confirmed in another hearing held on 24 March 1994 entitled *Human Rights and MFN*, before the International Security, International Organizations and Human Rights Subcommittees.[45] These subcommittees were looking for resolutions by using the MFN in monitoring the degree to which China abides by universal human rights. They were focusing on the following five conditions:

1. taking steps to begin adhering to the universal declaration of human rights;
2. releasing and providing an acceptable account for Chinese citizens imprisoned or detained for the nonviolent expression of their political and religious beliefs, including such expression of beliefs in connection with the Democracy Wall and Tiananmen Square movements;
3. ensuring humane treatment of prisoners, such as by allowing access to prisons by international humanitarian and human rights organizations;
4. protecting Tibet's distinctive religious and cultural heritage; and
5. permitting international radio and television broadcasts into China.[46]

The above-mentioned problems were exactly the major concerns of the United States. In fact, more human rights related problems such as the abuse of orphans in Shanghai, high death rate in orphanages, the debate over Asian values versus the universality of human rights and the imprisonment of Wei Jingsheng have been brought to the attention of the United States, too.[47] Nevertheless, in deciding to withdraw China's MFN status, the White House should also consider the huge possible economic caused by Chinese retaliation. A study carried out by the World Bank indicated that if MFN status were withdrawn in 1990, the sale of Chinese products to the United States would have been reduced by 43 from 139 to 96 percent, an all-or-nothing economic battle.[48]

In addition, it seemed that the facilitation of human rights recognition was not correctly maintained by using the MFN status as a monitoring measure. Eventually, the MFN ceased to be the leverage to monitor human rights in China when the linkage between human rights and MFN was dropped. The crux of the problem, as mentioned by the U.S. Department of State Human Rights Report in February 1995 was due to the fact that "The People's Republic of China is an authoritarian state in which the Chinese Communist Party monopolizes decision-making authority."[49]

The most important of all, nevertheless, is that the MFN issue provides a useful tool to facilitate U.S. foreign policy in shaping China toward a more market-oriented system. Therefore, the failure to grant MFN status to China, according to Laura D'Andrea Tyson, former chief economic adviser to President Clinton, "would prove not only ineffective, but counterproductive. It would impose substantial economic costs on the United States while jeopardizing China's peaceful transition to a more market-oriented, open society that respects the rule of law."[50]

Summary and Conclusion

From time to time, trade and economic relations have become the major issue of foreign relations between China and the United States in the post-cold war era. Trade, together with the huge Chinese market, acts as the major instrument for Chinese economic development. However, the Chinese ways of practicing trade and its perception toward trading activities are different from that of the international society. Moreover, the complexity of the Taiwan issue has been a pain in the neck of the Chinese government since 1949. Nevertheless, post-cold war Sino-American relations witnessed the continued granting of MFN status by the U.S. government, even though human rights improvement seems unnoticeable. The engagement of U.S. Chinese foreign policy, as explored, was confronted with many difficulties. However, if we use larger scales of measurement, such as marketization and China's involvement in the world economy, the picture of Sino-American divergence might be perceived from other convergent points of view. These points are what the next chapter will explore.

Notes

1. *United States-China Relations* 25, no. 1 (Summer 1996): 3.
2. David Strand, "Protest in Beijing: Civil Society and Public Sphere in China" *Problems of Communism* (May-June 1990): 1–19; Lawrence R. Sullivan, "The Emergence of Civil Society in China, Spring 1989" in *The Chinese People's Movement Perspectives on Spring 1989*, edited by Tony Seich (New York: M. E. Sharpe, Inc., 1990): 126–144 and Heath B. Chamberlain, " On the Search for Civil Society in China" *Modern China* 19, no. 2 (April 1993): 199–215.
3. *Beijing Review*, 21–27 October 1996, 14.
4. *The China Business Review* 23, no. 3 (May-June 1996): 41.
5. *South China Morning Post*, 23 June 1996.
6. *A Fragile Relationship* is the title of a book written by Harry Harding to illustrate foreign relations between China and the United States after 1972. The book details the uncertainties and the ups and downs of foreign relations between them. Harry Harding, *A Fragile Relationship: the United States and China Since 1972* (Washington, DC: The Brookings Institution, 1992).
7. William H. Overholt, *The Rise of China: How Economic Reform is Creating a New Superpower* (New York: W. W. Norton and Company, 1993), 415.
8. *International Herald Tribune*, 26 June 1996, 8.
9. *Financial Times*, 13 February 1995.
10. China's bilateral MFN treatment with the United States is restricted by the Jackson-Vanek amendment to the 1974 U.S. trade act, that required "annual presidential certification that China was not violating human rights by placing restrictions on emigration." It planted the seeds of antagonism between China and the United States in the renewal of MFN treatment on yearly bases. See Harold K. Jacobson and Michel Oksenberg, *China's Participation in the IMF, the World Bank, and GATT: Toward a Global Economic Order* (Ann Arbor, MI: The University of Michigan Press, 1990), 92.
11. Department of State, "Intellectual Property: Memorandum of Understanding Between the United States of America and the People's Republic of China," 17 January 1992, TIAS no. 12036, 8.
12. Ibid., 6.
13. U.S. General Accounting Office, *U.S.-China Trade: Implementation of Agreements on Market Access and Intellectual Property.* Report to the Honorable Hank Brown, U.S. Senate, January 1995, 7.
14. Ibid.
15. Ibid., 44.
16. Ibid.
17. Ibid., 45.
18. Ibid.
19. Ibid.
20. Ibid., 48.
21. Ibid.
22. Chang Wen, "Comments on the Case of Infringement on the MICROSOFT/MS-DOS Trademarks," *China Patents and Trademarks Quarterly* 3, no. 42 (July 1995), 88.
23. Ibid.

24. *China Law and Practice* 9, no. 3 (31 March 1995), 6.
25. *International Herald Tribune*, 18 June 1996, 1.
26. *International Herald Tribune*, 16 May 1996, 1.
27. Seth Faison, "China's New Anti-Piracy Drive Brings Results", *International Herald Tribune*, 8 April 1997, 16.
28. United States Information Service, *Foreign Policy Backgrounder*, "Lord: U.S. Seeks to Engage, Not Contain China" (5 July 1996): 1.
29. Joseph S. Nye, Jr., "The Case for Deep Engagement" *Foreign Affairs* 74, no. 4 (July/August 1995): 94.
30. USIS, "Lord: U.S. Seeks to Engage, Not Contain China," 5.
31. Section 1, Public Law 96-8 (22 U.S.C. 3301-3316), "Taiwan Relations Act," section 19. More details of the United States and Taiwan's foreign relations in terms of documentation can be located in Stephen P. Gilbert and William M. Carpenter, eds., *America and Island China: A Documentary History* (New York: University Press of America, 1989).
32. The whole amendment is as follows:

> Sec. 19. the Congress further finds and declares that there are no legitimate foreign policy grounds for preventing members of the government chosen by the people of Taiwan from making private visits to the United States. Accordingly, notwithstanding any other provision of law, no individual from the democratically elected leadership chosen by the people of Taiwan or their elected representatives may be excluded from the United States on the basis of a determination by the Secretary of State that the entry or proposed activities in the United States of such individual would have potentially serious adverse foreign policy consequences for the United States.

> The above-mentioned bill was introduced collectively by Mr. Torricelli, Mr. Gilman, Mr. Lantos, Mr. Gedjenson, Mr. Solomon, Mr. Ackermen, Mr. Rohrabacher, Mr. Faleomavaega, Mr. Brown of Ohio, Mr. Deutsch, and Ms. Pelosi in the House Committee on International Relations, H.R. 1460., 104th Cong., 1st sess., 6 April 1995.

33. *Far Eastern Economic Review*, 14 September 1995, 22.
34. The Taiwan Straits Exchange Foundation (SEF) and the Association for Relations Across the Taiwan Straits (ARATS) were established to settle their complex issues of unification. The first meeting was held in Singapore in 1993. However, they canceled the scheduled meetings after Lee's visit to Cornell, without announcing the date of resumption yet. See The Economic Intelligence Unit, *Country Report: Taiwan*, 3d quarter 1995, p.8.
35. The Economist, *The World in 1996*, 72.
36. Jaw-Ling Joanne Chang, "The U.S. Congress v. the White House: A Case Study of Most-Favored-Nation Status for the PRC, 1990–92" *EurAmerica* 23, no. 2 (June 1993): 9.
37. Ibid.
38. U.S. House Committee on Ways and Means, *Extension of MFN Status to Romania, Hungary, and the People's Republic of China: Hearing before the Subcommittee on Trade*, 97th Cong., 2d sess., 12 and 13 July 1982, 96.
39. Ibid., 97.
40. Nicholas R. Lardy, *China in the World Economy* (Washington, DC: Institute for International Economics, 1994): 99.
41. U.S. House Committee of Foreign Affairs, Subcommittee on the Human Rights and International Organization, *MFN Status for China: Hearing before the Subcommittee of the Asian and Pacific Affairs*, 29 May and 26 June 1991.

42. Ibid., 2.
43. Ibid., 7.
44. Ibid., 8.
45. U.S. House Committee of Foreign Affairs, *Human Rights and MFN: Hearing before the International Security, International Organizations and Human Rights Subcommittee*, 104th Cong., 24 March 1994.
46. Ibid., 7–8.
47. *China Rights Forum* (Spring 1996): 4–31; *China Rights Forum* (Fall 1996): 32–35 and *China Rights Forum* (Spring 1997): 10–13.
48. Nicholas R. Lardy, *China in the World Economy*, 102.
49. U.S. Department of State, *Human Rights Report, China*, February 1995, 1.
50. Laura D'Andrea Tyson, "Beyond MFN," *Asian Wall Street Journal*, 29 May 1997, 6.

9

U.S. Foreign Policy Convergences with China

> *Our Policy will seek to facilitate a peaceful evolution*
> *of China from communism to democracy....*[1]
> —Warren Christopher

Introduction

In relations between China and the United States, the salience of the context of augmented market liberalism (AML) rests on the use of some structured arrangements[2] of the world economy as tools of American foreign policy to bring about change within China. The more China becomes internationalized, the more easily it could be transformed by American foreign policy—to a market economy.[3] In addition, the United States is the organizer and the architect of the chessboard for the international players of whom China is just one. This was so, whether in the cold war period or in the post-cold war era.[4]

Relations between the United States and China are complicated. Neither the power-centric model nor the institutional framework model is sufficient for understanding their unique relationship,[5] especially during the post-cold war era. The instruments of U.S. containment policy during the cold war are not adequate enough to depict the whole picture of their foreign relations, particularly now when China is becoming more open and active in the international arena. As China becomes more economically developed, the IPE expands our analysis to include the economic aspects of their relationship. The shift from a containment policy to economic pacification enables us to reexamine the usefulness of those long-established regimes (international organizations and economic institutions) in analyzing contemporary Sino-American relations.[6]

This chapter attempts to highlight some of the implications which derive from the above. The internationalization of China has, at least, three implications.

1. A large socialist developing country has a chance of being involved in the structured world economic organizations which were predominantly organized by the capitalist states.
2. From the viewpoint of international economy, the involvement of China in global economic organizations paves the way for the United States to monitor China's trade pattern within the structured world economy.
3. The claim to the status of a developing country has been affected as China becomes more economically developed and participates more actively in world economy.

These three implications will be discussed as follows. They are important in the sense that not only the historical understandings of power relations between nations needs to be reevaluated, but also the ingredients that underlie the concept of the "rise of China" demand reinterpretation as well.

Implication of China's Involvement in the World Economy

The first implication is that a "large, underdeveloped, closed"[7] and socialist country like China has a chance to be involved in the world economy. This is intertwined with the change in the whole environment and the argument of a theoretical change in international relations that underpin the foreign policies of the United States. This argument will be illustrated by analyzing the explanation given by realist observers of the changing pattern of Sino-U.S. relations, who take into account the variations of American foreign policy as well as the shape of the structured world economy. This perspective is generated by the assumption of the realist school on the one hand, and the empirical findings of Chinese compliance with the legal norms required by the United States on the other. Among the realist thinkers, Hans J. Morgenthau was one of the most renowned. His six principles of political realism[8] dominated the whole tone of U.S. foreign policy after World War II. His realist approach, derived from a mass of historical evidence and observations, enables us to grasp the underlying relations among nations. Nevertheless, the applicability of the pure realist approach to the relations between China and the United States is far from satisfying.

Although I am not able, nor even capable, to criticize the whole school of realism, nevertheless, it seems that the theory is insufficient for analyzing the relations between China and the United States. Recent developments between these two countries suggest that the fifth principle of the realist school—"political realism refuses to identify the moral aspirations of a particular nation with the moral laws that govern the universe"[9]—is gravely challenged by their negotiation in the areas of trade in general and intellectual property rights in particular.

As far as trade issues are concerned, China has been waiting for re-entry into GATT since 1986.[10] If China were a GATT member, it would have to abide by the rules of the game. That is to say, the international moral principle of trade issues should be observed by those countries which are involved in the international economy. On 1 January 1995, GATT was replaced by the WTO, which is said to be more powerful in legal enforcement and trade negotiation. Furthermore, with reference to the intellectual property rights agreement reached on 26 February 1995, China has to "take immediate steps to address rampant piracy throughout China and to make long-term changes to ensure effective enforcement of intellectual property rights."[11] Then, if China can be forced to observe the law and act accordingly, the final outcome, to a certain extent, would be a concrete repudiation of Morgenthau's theory, at least the fifth principle.[12]

From this perspective, the real situation between the United States and China is far more complex than can be appreciated by a solely power-centric model. Instead, following the perspective of a U.S. constructed world economy, the particular relations between China and the United States are alterable as long as the world economy provides an arena of change. If the realist school sets an absolute standard for measuring the interactions among nations, the neorealist thinker allows a little more room for widening our scope by taking into account the social setting that shapes the world at large. This idea has been clearly depicted by Kenneth N. Waltz, who has argued that "Man is born and in his natural condition remains neither good nor bad. It is society that is the degrading force in men's lives..."[13] If society can modify the state of nature of human beings, by the same token, a great constitution of people, the state, is alterable when the international economy and environment change. Thus, China's modernization and developmental processes are greatly and positively associated with the policies of the United States. But the consequent results and the necessary changes in legal systems, laws of property rights, market openness, relaxation of regulations and so on should be taken into consideration if we want to understand how China is being modified and transformed by U.S. foreign policy under the framework of AML.

The entry of China into the world economy matches George Modelski's idea of foreign policy: "the system of activities evolved by communities for changing the behaviour of other states and for adjusting their own activities to the international environment."[14] Since the world economy is structured by the web of U.S. foreign policy, it necessarily affects the development of Chinese foreign policy.

To analyze the behavior of nations according to the power-centric model is relatively easier than by using a normative concept such as cooperation. If Sino-U.S. relations are changing from a pure power-centric model to a new model,[15] does it necessarily mean that they are tending to be more cooperative in the future? To cooperate means many things. What kind of cooperation do they want? To what extent can the two countries cooperate? If the two countries cooperate, what are the implications for other countries? First, cooperation should imply mutual benefits as well as recognitions.[16] For instance, China's abiding by the rules set by the United States should not be detrimental to the fundamental interests of China. On the contrary, the acceptance of the rules may result in the realization of its other foreign objectives. As Robert Keohane put it, intergovernmental cooperation "takes place when the policies actually followed by one government are regarded by its partners as facilitating realization of their own objectives, as the result of a process of policy coordination."[17] In other words, observance of international standards in terms of property rights and trade agreements may help China realize its objectives of economic development and modernization. Nevertheless, any further cooperation between them would require opening of the U.S. market and the relaxation of trade barriers in China, as well as a peaceful settlement of their disputes. If conflicts are embedded in the relations between the two countries, the task of cooperation lies in the establishment of an institution to prevent the possible escalation of conflict. Now, we will examine the second implication of why it is necessary for the United States to monitor China in the world economy.

Implications of the United States Monitoring China in the World Economy

In general, the rapprochement of China with the United States and its nest of world policy constructions can be divided into the following.

First, the postwar economy saw an American-dominated international economic environment which was initiated by the establishment of a U.S. international economy.[18] Second, this milieu conditioned the reach of American foreign policy, without much obstruction from the rest of the world. Third, building from this foundation of a self-established superpower, the U.S. foreign policy changed in accordance with its perception of change in the socialist movement. In other words, the economic burden shifted to other countries which demanded American dollars in the hope of redevelopment and a favorable gold standard monetary system. The less the restriction on economic matters, the more the room for more persistence of foreign policies. Fourth, the collapse of the monetary system paved the way for a change in U.S. foreign policy. In 1971, the "coincidence" of the formal breakdown of the Bretton Woods system and the secret visit of Security Adviser Henry Kissinger to China, followed by a formal visit by President Nixon in 1972, reinforces my argument that a change in the international monetary system prompted the United States to alter its foreign policy towards China. The containment policy was precipitately abandoned, and the U.S. policy shifted to establishing a less hostile and more cooperative relationship with China. Finally, the open door policy adopted by China in 1978[19] and its deepening involvement in the world economy highlighted the success of U.S. foreign policy objective: to change China.

In other words, the international arena was awash with the elements that contributed to the construction of the cold war. But, here it will be argued that if the United States was not so wealthy and had not been so dominated by the international monetary system, it would not have been so easy for other countries to lean to one side in support of U.S. containment policy.[20] On the contrary, when the Bretton Woods system collapsed on 15 August 1971, although somewhat reluctantly, the United States[21] accepted the change in the international arena regarding the cold war as well as the dominance of American foreign policy. Nixon's dramatic visit to China in February 1972 provides strong evidence in support of the argument that suggests a relationship between economic power and foreign policy orientation.

Unfortunately, the transformation of China from a backward country to a relatively modernized one created dilemmas. These were not because of the *absolute* decline in U. S. power, but because of its *relative* decline. The United States, in a sense, now has to talk to and make sometimes unsatisfactory compromises with other countries sometimes in an unsatisfactory manner because of the weakening of its hegemonic power. Since a hegemony tries to maintain stability in the world economy through its revolving power of bestowing punishment and giving rewards,[22] the emerging power of China could (from the viewpoint of the United States) challenge its hegemonic status.[23] For example, many are skeptical that a "Greater China," which combines Hong Kong, Taiwan, and Macao with China, will surpass the United States and Japan in the early part of the year 2000.[24] In terms of countries with a trade surplus with the United States, China ranks second, after Japan—its trade surplus with the United States is $29,494 million.[25] These alarming facts affect U.S. policy towards China.[26]

If the United States tries to accommodate China in a way in which it enables it to have continuing monitoring power over it, and is able to ensure that the stability of the world economy will not be disturbed by the sudden emergence of China as well as a world economic force, its foreign policy and strategy have to be changed. In other words, it must resolve the dilemma without affecting its own national interest nor the stability of the world economy. The mid-1994 delinking of human rights issues from the MFN status is evidence of this approach.[27] The subsequent negotiation and talks between the trade representatives of the two countries in Februrary and March 1995 were evidence of the success in pursuing a consciously formulated economic strategy.[28] Progress was made when China agreed to comply with the law made by the United States and agreed to abide by the agreement and deal with the violation of intellectual property rights.[29] The idea that economic issues should be delinked from human rights and that the United States should concentrate on finding a feasible solution to economic and trade issues to change China, comes very close to Goldstein and Keohane's recent work *Ideas and Foreign Policy*.[30] As long as ideas become the "beliefs held by individuals,"[31] the "political outcomes, particularly those related to foreign policy"[32] can be realized through an appropriate foreign policy strategy. Furthermore, if one idea is pursued and can be realized through a foreign policy objective, it would be possible to spread this idea to many other areas, and lower level commercial cooperation to higher level cooperation. The following quote from an editorial comment entitled "Ideas Follow Trade" in the *International Herald Tribune* spells out this "idea" precisely:

But if the idea of orderly law enforcement takes hold in purely commercial areas—such as curbing theft of copyrighted movies, music and computer programs—

it may spread. It may begin to affect Chinese attitudes in two other subjects of great importance to the rest of the world, arms control and human rights.[33]

In the following section, the third implication of China's Third World role in the international arena will be discussed.

Implication of China's Third World Role in the World Economy

Dr. Harry Harding, in a 1995 satellite interview with participants from Hong Kong, Taiwan, Seoul, Tokyo, and Singapore, commented that "China is not a developing country, neither is she a developed one."[34] The basic question of what China is remains unanswered. The implications of China's Third World role are important. A clear-cut Third World identity for China would ease many problems relating to trade negotiations with the rest of the world, on the one hand, and between China and other Third World countries—conflicting in scrambling for world resources or cooperating in creating a New International Economic Order (NIEO)—on the other.

The following section illustrates the perceptions of decision makers with respect to China's Third World role. It then goes on to demonstrate that the position of China's Third World status is in fact an ambiguous issue. Consequently, China's membership in the Group of 77, its capture of international loans, and even the applicability of a new measurement of development, Purchasing Power Parity (PPP), become bones of contention between China and other Third World countries. Let us first go back to 1954.

Decision Makers' Perceptions of China's Third World Status

In 1954, Chinese Premier Zhou Enlai was the first to introduce the objective of making the Five Principles of Peaceful Coexistence the basis for future foreign policy negotiations.[35] The Bandung Conference held in Indonesia in 1955 paved the way for China to present its envisaged Third World role in that forum. Although there were differences among the participating countries on China's claim to Third World status,[36] the category of being a Third World country was still valid at that time. The Third World role of China was also carefully delineated in Mao Zedong's theory of three worlds (*San fen shi jei lun*).[37]

Mao's theory derived from his perception of the world economy.[38] To him, First World countries were the United States and the Soviet Union; the Second World included Japan, Canada, the United Kingdom, and European countries; and the Third World included Asian and Latin American countries and China.[39] Since all Third World countries were being exploited by the imperialism and hegemony of the First World, they should come together so as to prevent further oppression by the First World. Besides, he thought the Second World, when pressured by the First World, could be encouraged to join the Third World to struggle against the First World in the long run.[40] Mao's theory was a mirror image of his long-held strategy of world revolution. The major objective was to create a united front of countries feeling exploited, to attack the First World.[41]

However, Mao's theory was not feasible. First, his definition of the Third World was solely based on ideology, without taking note of the realistic economic nature of each country. Second, the self-fulfilling concept of three worlds clashed with the individual self-interest of countries in their economic development instead of ideological confrontation. This was particularly true of the developing countries of Asia. Finally, the theory suffered a serious setback when Mao died on 9 September 1976. The leader of the generation, Deng Xiaoping, placed more emphasis on economic development than on continuous ideological struggle.

Deng emphasized economic development, North-South relations, and even South-South cooperation. According to him, "resolving this [North-South] problem should rely on North-South dialogue, I advocate North-South dialogue."[42] Contrary to Mao's logic, Deng's open-door policy resulted in China's attraction of First World and Second World countries rather than counteracting them. With regard to economic development and standard of living, China benefited rather than suffered from dealing with the First World—for instance, in its 1986 reapplication to GATT and in talks with the United States over MFN issues and violation of intellectual property rights. Mao's three-worlds theory formally broke down at the United Nations' Forty-third Conference on 20 September 1988, when Foreign Minister Qian Qichen of China announced openly that "the world was going towards multipolarization."[43] In fact, multipolarity of the world economy and the perception of the Chinese government of its role in the world contradicted China's self-proclaimed status as a Third World country.

To conclude this discussion of decision makers' perspectives of China's Third World status, we should pay very close attention to Premier Li Peng's speech at the United Nations on 31 January 1992. Li Peng made an unmistakable distinction between China and the Third World: "the developing countries whose population constitutes the overwhelming majority of the world's total are finding *themselves* in an increasingly difficult position (emphasis added)."[44] The use of *themselves* and not ourselves (whether a Freudian slip or not) qualifies as clustering Third World countries on the one hand, and China on the other. In a word, the decision maker's self-portrait position of China as neither developed nor developing is emerging upon the arena of world politics.

Bones of Contention with The Third World

China's future relations with the Third World will be strained, if not confrontational, especially on the following issues.

First, China is not a member of Group of 77.[45] The establishment of Group of 77 (after the 1964 United Nations Conference on Trade and Development at Geneva, [UNCTAD]) constituted the biggest movement of developing countries hoping to create a new world order with an international economy more favorable to them. However, China's absence from this vital group means the loss of a forum in which to discuss concrete cooperation and dialogue with the Third World.

Second, as long as China is moving towards economic prosperity, the conflicts with the Third World are substantial. According to Samuel Kim, "By 1989 China had become the world's largest recipient of official development assistance from all sources ($2,153 million)."[46] Again, the State Administration of Foreign Exchange Control (SAFEC) announced that China's outstanding debt at the end of 1993 was U.S.$83.5 billion.[47] According to an official OECD publication, China's considerable debt created no problem at all because "its [China's] solid economic performance should prevent it [China] from facing solvency or liquidity problems."[48] In terms of international lending and financing, China's image of loan-snatching becomes an area of dispute with developing countries rather than an opportunity for cohesion. Despite Deng's advocacy of South-South economic cooperation, the fact that China is the largest debtor among developing countries makes China's future policies with them uneasy.

Finally, the fundamental question of whether China is a Third World nation or not is challenged when PPP[49] is applied, instead of the traditional gross domestic product (GDP) per capita, to measure the standard of living in China. For example, China's GDP per capita in March 1995 was $435 (using traditional GDP calculations), but using PPP pushes the figures up to $2,428.[50] That's a colossal increase of 550 percent! Although it should be argued that the application of PPP is, sometimes, exaggerated as in the case of many developing countries,[51] continuing research on finding a parity rate of exchange and on refining the techniques in measuring exchange rate and inflation would result in a more precise estimation of living standards in developing countries, particularly China.[52] In other words, the increasing internationalization of China and opening of its economy would make the PPP a more precise and appropriate unit of measurement.

At this level, China's Third World status and its foreign policy are still covered by a veil of ambiguity. One might conclude by saying that "Beijing no longer asserted that the Chinese model of economic development or political organization were necessarily appropriate for developing states, but maintained that pragmatic mutually beneficial economic relations were the central hallmark of Chinese-Developing World relations."[53] In addition, coupled with the above arguments, China's Third World relations and policies towards "other Third World nations" served a functional role in the early years: for Mao, an ideological function and for Deng, a developmental function. However, as time goes by, when China can handle more smoothly the issue of its ambiguous relationship to and within the Third World, policies towards the Third World will become expandable. That is why the incorporation of China into the world economy and the function of U.S. policy towards China become important: to analyze its developmental trends as well as monitor China according to standards of the world economy.

Conclusion

It has been argued that the United States and China's foreign relations are not static as they were in the cold war era. Nor have they become hostile, especially if we look at their trade and continuous negotiations. The post-cold war era required a functional change of the long-established economic institutions in accordance with China's internationalization process and economic development. Sino-U.S. relations reveal that in theory and in reality, the IPE is being subordinated to U.S. policy toward China. The phenomenon in the international society is the result of interaction among different countries, whether socialist or capitalist. A farewell to the cold war does not mean that we should neglect the power relations among nations. In fact, reexamining pure power concepts is essential to an understanding of U.S.-China relations. Internationalization of socialist China into the world economy, monitoring China's compliance with international rules, and China's Third World role all combine to create new implications for future U.S-China relations. In the final chapter, the transformative process of AML will be substantiated accordingly.

Notes

1. This is one of the statements made by Warren Christopher, Secretary of State-Designate of the United States during his confirmation hearings on 13 January 1993. See William H. Overholt, *The Rise of China: How Economic Reform is Creating a New Superpower* (New York and London: W. W. Norton and Company, 1993): 365.

2. A structured world economy refers to the world organizations, especially GATT or the WTO, the IMF, and the IBRD or World Bank, that were established under the auspices of the United States.

3. Actually, the idea of transformation is premature if we look at some of the comments on Clinton's new policy towards China. David Zweig has argued that "Yet, if the United States does not press the Chinese to adopt democratic institutions for China's own benefit, China will continue its cycle of liberalizations and crackdowns, which alienate the population and undermine economic growth." See David Zweig, "Clinton and China: Creating a Policy Agenda that Works," *Current History* 92, no. 575 (September 1993): 246.

4. The contending theories of the hegemonic power of the United States is still being debated between Joseph S. Nye and Paul Kennedy. Nevertheless, the reality is that Chinese internationlization and its involvement in the world economy clearly moved it to the structured regimes which were initiated by the United States after World War II. See Joseph S. Nye, Jr., *Bound to Lead: The Changing Nature of American Power* (New York: Basic Books, 1990) and Paul Kennedy, *The Rise and Fall of the Great Powers: Economic Change and Military Conflict from 1500 to 2000* (London: Fontana Press, 1989).

5. With reference to the subject matter of international political economy (IPE), Susan Strange is more inclined to defines it as "...social, political and economic arrangements" that derive from "...man-made institutions and sets of self-set rules and customs." See Susan Strange, *States and Markets*, 2d ed., (London: Pinter Publishers, 1994): 18. While Robert Keohane is more concerned with power relations, he has defined the IPE as "the intersection of the substantive area studied by economics—production and exchange of marketable means of want satisfaction—with the process by which power is exercised that is central to politics." See Robert O. Keohane, *After Hegemony: Cooperation and Discord in the World Political Economy* (Princeton, NJ: Princeton University Press, 1984): 21.

6. Here, I emphasize formal institutional matters, a little bit more although regimes might refer to institutional things or noninstitutional matters. Nevertheless, they all converged on the "cooperative behavior" and opportunity of cooperative behavior between the United States and China. Moreover, the "structure" and "scope" of those regimes play a transformatory role allowing China to participate easily or not in those organizations. See Stephan Haggard and Beth A. Simmons, "Theories of International Regimes" *International Organization* 41, no. 3 (Summer 1987): 495–97.

7. These categorizations are provided by James N. Rosenau. See James N. Rosenau, "Pre-Theories and Theories of Foreign Policy" in John A. Vasquez, ed *Classics of International Relations,* 2d ed., (Englewood Cliffs, NJ: Prentice-Hall, 1990): 168.

8. The six principles are as follows:
   1. Political realism believes that politics, like society in general, is governed by objective laws that have their roots in human nature;
   2. The main signpost that helps political realism to find its way through the landscape of international politics is the concept of interest defined in terms of power;
   3. Realism assumes that its key concept of interest defined as power is an objective category which is universally valid, but it does not endow that concept with a meaning that is fixed once and for all;
   4. Political realism is aware of the moral significance of political action;
   5. Political realism refuses to identify the moral aspirations of a particular nation with the moral laws that govern the universe; and,
   6. The difference, then, between political realism and other schools of thought is real, and it is profound.

   These principles are contained in Morgenthau's book. See Hans J. Morgenthau, *Politics Among Nations: the Struggle for Power and Peace* (brief ed. rev. Kenneth W. Thompson) (New York: McGraw-Hill, Inc., 1993): 4–16.

9. Ibid., 13.

10. China joined the IMF and the World Bank in 1980, and began to apply for full membership in GATT in 1986. See Harold K. Jacobson and Michel Oksenberg, *China's Participation in the IMF, the World Bank, and GATT: Toward a Global Economic Order* (Ann Arbor, MI: University of Michigan Press, 1990).

11. USIS, *News Release,* 2 March 1995, 2.

12. After four hours of continuous negotiations between the United States trade representative Mickey Kantor and his Chinese counterparts, further movement towards admission to the WTO was ensured provided China followed a "flexible, pragmatic and realistic basis." See *South China Morning Post* (Hong Kong), 13 March 1995, 1.

13. Kenneth N. Waltz, *Man, the State and War: A Theoretical Analysis* (New York: Columbia University Press, 1959): 4–5.

14. Mahendra Kumar, *Theoretical Aspects of International Politics,* 3d ed., (Agra: Shiva Lal Agarwala and Company, 1975): 310.

15. Harry Harding, *A Fragile Relationship: The United States and China Since 1972* (Washington, DC: Brookings Institution, 1992). Besides, he also mentioned in an interview that the new United States and China relations are "neither friend nor enemy." A more "realistic and mature relations should be established between them." See *Hong Kong Economic Journal Monthly* 17, no. 9 (December 1993): 12–17.

16. Mutual recognition is like reciprocity. If country A protects its goods, country B would do in the same manner, and vice versa. See Joshua S. Goldstein, *International Relations* (New York: HarperCollins College Publishers, 1994): 335–37.

17. Robert O. Keohane, *After Hegemony: Cooperation and Discord in the World Political Economy* (Princeton, NJ: Princeton University Press, 1984): 51–52.

18. Susan Strange, "The Future of the American Empire" in Richard Little and Michael Smith, eds., *Perspectives on World Politics,* 2d. ed., (London: Routledge, 1991): 434–43.

19. The open door policy adopted after the Third Plenum of the Eleventh Party Congress in 1978 paved the way for China and its citizens to experience the

fresh air in the world economy, having the opportunity to look back and strive for the future.

20. U.S. monetary power was securely established after the meeting of those major powers at Bretton Woods, New Hampshire in July 1944. The aim was to formulate a monetary system which could ease forthcoming monetary problems confronting different countries. To put it simply, the U.S. was the guarantor who was responsible for the conversion of U.S. $35 to one ounce of gold if the demand arose. Since there was one and only one country—the United States—which was sufficiently credible to be the linchpin, the U.S. dollar became the golden child between the 1950s and the early 1960s. U.S. foreign policy was strongly related to its credit-worthiness at that time. See Joan Edelman Spero, *The Politics of International Economic Relations*, 4th. ed., (London: St. Martin's Press, Inc., 1990): 31–48.

21. Directly quoted from Robert Gilpin. He said "The American government was under pressure to convert tens of billions of dollars into gold, and the international monetary system was threaten to break down." See Robert Gilpin, *The Political Economy of International Relations* (Princeton, NJ: Princeton University Press, 1987): 140. For more details, especially the technical terms and the subtle elements of Bretton Woods System, see John S. Hodgson and Mark G. Herander, *International Economic Relations* (Englewood Cliffs, NJ: Prentice-Hall, Inc., 1983): 381–96.

22. Robert Gilpin, ibid., 75.

23. Susan Strange, *The Future of the American Empire*, 56–57.

24. *Newsweek* 121, no. 7, 15 February 1993, 12–13.

25. USIS, *News Release*, 21 February 1995, 3.

26. Apart from the astonishing book written by William H. Overholt, *The Rise of China: How Economic Reform is Creating a New Superpower* (New York and London: W. W. Norton and Company, 1993) there are many recent books dealing with the same topic—the rise of China. They are Maurice Brosseau and Lo Chi Kin, eds., *China Review 1994* (Hong Kong: The Chinese University Press, 1994), Denis Dwyer, *China: The Next Decades* (London: Longman Scientific and Technical, 1994) and Susumu Yabuki, *China's New Political Economy: The Giant Awakes* (trans. Stephan M. Harner) (Boulder, CO: Westview Press, 1995).

27. *Hong Kong Economic Journal*, 24 May 1994, 30, and 27 May 1994, 6. and *Ming Pao* (Hong Kong), 28 March 1994, A11.

28. *International Herald Tribune*, 1 March 1995, 6.

29. USIS, *News Release*, 2 March 1995, 2–5. and *South China Morning Post* (Hong Kong), 13 March 1995, 1.

30. Judith Goldstein and Robert O. Keohane, eds., *Ideas and Foreign Policy: Beliefs, Institutions, and Political Change* (Ithaca, NY: Cornell University Press, 1993).

31. Ibid., 3.

32. Ibid.

33. *International Herald Tribune*, 16 March 1995, 6.

34. The satellite interview took place in Washington, DC. I was one of the participants from Hong Kong watching the one-hour broadcast at the American Embassy.

35. Zhou announced this at the First National People's Congress. The five principles are: (1) mutual respect for sovereignty and territorial integrity; (2) mutual nonaggression; (3) noninterference in each other's internal affairs; (4) equality and mutual benefit; and (5) peaceful coexistence.

36. Lillian Craig Harris and Robert L. Worden, eds., *China and the Third World: Champion or Challenger?* (Dover: Auburn House Publishing Company, 1986): 2–3.

37. Kwok-sing Li (Comp.), *A Glossary of Political Terms of The People's Republic of China*, trans. Mary Lok, (Hong Kong: The Chinese University Press, 1995): 363.
38. Mao's three worlds theory was first introduced in a meeting with Zambia's president on 22 February 1974. See Kwok-sing Li, ibid., 363.
39. Kwok-sing Li, ibid., 363 and also see Forty *Years of Chinese Communist Party Rule* (Beijing: Chinese Communist Party Data Publishing House, August 1989): 375.
40. John W. Garver, *Foreign Relations of the People's Republic of China* (Englewood Cliffs, New Jersey: Prentice-Hall, 1993): 166–67.
41. *A Great Dictionary concerning Mao Zedong* (Guangxi: Guangxi renmin chubanshe, 1992): 1017–18.
42. *Deng Xiaoping Wenxuan*, vol. 3 (Beijing: Renmin chubanshe, 1993): 56.
43. See Kwok-sing Li, *A Glossary*, 364; *Xinhua News Agency Bulletin*, 22 September and 7 October 1988.
44. Li Peng, "Chinese Views on a New World Order", *Beijing Review* 35, no. 7, 17 February 1992, 8.
45. Robert E. Riggs and Jack C. Plano, *The United Nations: International Organization and World Politics*, 2d ed., (Belmont, CA: Wadsworth Publishing Company, 1994): 62.
46. Samuel S. Kim, ed., *China and the World: Chinese Foreign Relations in the Post-Cold War Era* (Boulder, CO: Westview Press, 1994): 154.
47. *China Economic Digest* (Hanli Consultancy Ltd., London), Autumn Issue, 1994, 15.
48. There are three countries: China, Indonesia and Malaysia. See The OECD Observer, no.184 (October/November 1993): 14.
49. The Purchasing Power Parity (PPP) theory is defined as "A theory which states that the exchange rate between one currency and another is an equilibrium when their domestic purchasing powers at that rate of exchange are equivalent" See G. Bannock, R. E. Baxter and R. Rees, *The Penguin Dictionary of Economics*, 3d ed., (London: Penguin Books, 1984): 362.
50. *Asiaweek* 21, no. 12, 24 March 1995, 53.
51. For example, India's GDP per capita was $310, and Bangladesh's was $220. The application of PPP leads to an increase of $1,126 and $1,290, respectively. See ibid., Paul A. Samuelson in his famous textbook *Economics* has argued in a similar way that the PPP technique for measuring living standards in developing countries results in a big differences from the traditional market measurement. See Paul A. Samuelson and William D. Nordhaus, *Economics*, 15th ed., (New York: McGraw-Hill, Inc., 1995): 671.
52. This is a very important definition, both politically and economically. In terms of politics, if China carries on its Third World status, it would easily receive trade concessions and special treatment from its trading counterparts, like other developing countries. Otherwise it would become a shield of protection against the rough sea of international trade activities, similar to "infant-industry" excuse using by many NICs in the 1970s. Economically, the search for a scientific and impartial definition helps in finding a good scale for estimating standard of living across national boundaries.
53. Daniel S. Papp, *Contemporary International Relations: Frameworks for Understanding*, 4th ed., (New York: Macmillan, 1994): 365

Part Five

Conclusions

10

The Market Force and China's Transformation

Although there are various disputes, problems, and differences between China and the United States, relations between the two countries must eventually be improved.[1]
—Deng Xiaoping

This chapter is a conclusion and projection of Sino-American relations throughout the cold war and the post-cold war era by dissecting the facilitation of market force. Augmented market liberalism, the U.S. policy toward China, is a cornerstone of their relations; China's market economy was induced partly by U.S. foreign policy. This study enables us not only to look at their bilateral foreign policy from the traditional diplomatic angle but also enlarges the perspective to include the macro structure under the facilitation of international political economy.

AML's Engendering Forces of Change

Military expansion and economic development coexisted in the world after World War II. NATO, the Truman Doctrine, the Korean War, and the Vietnam War were products of the cold war. Nevertheless, international economic relations facilitated the establishment of the GATT, IMF, the World Bank and numerous international organizations at the same time. Those international organizations were not the byproducts of containment; instead they were important pillars resulting from U.S. efforts to build economic development and cooperation among countries. U.S. foreign policy initiatives had the market force as an important variable. U.S. foreign policy toward China, engendered under those international circumstances, created a momentum for change.

The encroachment of Japan by U.S. foreign policy after World War II nurtured an international environment conducive to the market economy. The encroachment of Japan's economic as well as political structure enabled the U.S. to safeguard capitalism from socialism. By the same token, the embankment of the Four Little Dragons with AML demonstrated the effectiveness and efficiency of the market force to transform countries. This process coincided with Alfred D. Chandler's argument on the market force's ability to transform societies. The Four Little Dragons' ties with the United States rejuvenated their economies and led to them gradually joining the world economy through trade and investment.

The U.S. policy of AML toward China was less successful in the 1950s and 1960s. On the one hand, China's domestic political atmosphere was a tainted ideology of struggle and socialism which prevented Mao from looking at the market potential of strong Sino-American relations. On the other hand, there was the cold war fear that encircled the world economy. Sino-American relations, particularly before 1972, were also part of the strategic triangle with the Soviet Union.

The economic nature of U.S. policy toward China becomes evident in an examination of Nixon's visit to China in 1972. Market force was facilitated during his visit by the downfall of the gold standard. Moreover, the market force actually shaped Nixon's visit as illustrated in chapter 6 by the statistics of wheat trading before and after the visit.

If Nixon's visit was said to be the breakthrough of Sino-American relations, the normalization process also witnessed a substantial shift in the context of U.S. power, from that of a single hegemonic force to its use of international regimes as a tool to extend its influence. China's industrial development, economic openness, internationalization, and increase in trade after 1978 came at a time when the world had already moved toward a relatively mature and sophisticated market economy. As Alexander Gerschenkron argued, "The more advanced the world economy, the greater the entry costs."[2] Many rules of conduct had been installed by international regimes such as WTO, the World Bank, and IMF. For China to fit into this structure required a big adjustment in its domestic, economic, and political policies. The guiding principle of the international regime, therefore, not only affected China's policy but also inherited the facilitation of the U.S. interests because support of free trade and political liberalization became America's "conviction."[3]

The post-cold war U.S. policy toward China was engagement and enlargement. There were both policy divergences and policy convergences. Intellectual property rights, Taiwan, and MFN status became areas of dispute. China's involvement in the world economy, the U.S. monitoring of China in the world economy, and China's role in the Third World were instances where policy converged. For the future, China's policy is oriented toward the market economy.

China's Development Trajectory and Policy Orientation

China's development was fundamentally molded by the market force. It resembles the path depicted in figure 10.1.

FIGURE 10.1
China's Path of Economic Development

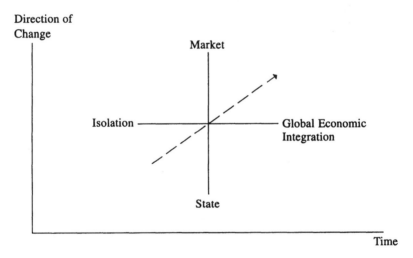

As time went on, the movement toward economic development and market openness became distinctive. The following sections will put forward my argument that the market force has fundamentally effected change in China's empirical context.

Fundamental Changes

The Communist Party added the market ingredient to China's Constitution, which became an inherent part of future Chinese policy-making. The constitutional amendments were made at the First Session of the Eighth National People's Congress on 29 March 1993. Perhaps, the most important was the statement "The state practices socialist market economy," which was added to Article 7.[4] Subsequently, in October 1993, political theorists of China's government including Ma Hung published *What is Socialist Market Economy?* The book served as a guiding principle and a formal testament to China's pursuit of a market economy.[5] As analyzed in chapter 8, the Chinese effort to join the WTO entailed a fundamental adaptation to the market and attention to the entrepreneurial system, the legal system, and a change in the context of economic planning.[6] We shall study these changes in turn.

Entrepreneurial System

Although the existence of state-run industries symbolizes China's communism and socialism, these industries have long been inefficient and ineffective. At the Fifth Session of the Eighth National People's Congress (NPC) and the Chinese People's Political Consultative Conference (CPPCC) in February 1997, delegates called for "a quick structural readjustment of China's manufacturing industry."[7] Jiang Zemin also promised "to strengthen management of the market and establish a better market framework."[8] This reform in Shanghai, for example, will leave 290,000 workers unemployed, complained Xu Kuangdi, the mayor of Shanghai, although it is in line with Shanghai's plan to upgrade its industries and become an international financial center.[9] The move indicates that the forthcoming Chinese economy will consider market competition to be the most important ingredient. Actually, the reform of state industries witnessed the movement toward the adaptation to the market economy. Some Chinese state industries went public in the Hong Kong stock exchange market under the categories of Shanghai A and B and Shenzhen A and B. Chinese stocks even outperformed other Asian stocks recently. For example, Shanghai A and B and Shenzhen A and B ranked the highest four indices in the Pacific Rim, having returns from 60.74 percent to 23.54 percent.[10]

The Market System

After the 1978 reform, the Chinese economy was overhauled. Development based on production and consumption swiftly energized nearly every sector of the country. China witnessed two major booms in her consumption demand, in 1985–86 and 1987–88.[11] With the rise in income levels, there was a steady drop in the purchase of foodstuffs and an increase in the consumption of durable goods and services such as washing machines, refrigerators, color televisions, and sewing machines.[12] However, since the Chinese economy is still governed by the macro-adjustments of the state, the price levels do not necessarily reflect the genuine market price. For example, the inflation rate and the consumer price rate might not truly reflect the consumption level.[13] Only when deregulation and privatization of state enterprises is fully implemented can genuine consumption levels be measured accurately.

The Legal System: Taxation Reform

Major tax reform was introduced along with market socialism at the Third Plenum of the Fourteenth National Congress from November 11–14 November 1993. The focus of this meeting was the "Decision of Some Issues Concerning the Establishment of a Socialist Market Economy."[14] A ten-chapter communiqué of ten chapters was issued immediately after the meeting. It can be categorized according to three aspects: (1) development of a better market structure; (2) acceleration of macro-economic control; and (3) reformation of state-enterprises.[15] Among others, reformation of taxation was one of the major topics.

The whole concept behind the tax reform was summarized by Liu Zhongli, the minister of finance:

> The financial and taxation reform to be launched next year [1 January 1994] is an important component of the establishment of a social market economic structure and a major measure vital to the country's long-term stability and order and future economic development, as well as reform of the economic structure as a whole.[16]

The reform *per se* is meant to generate a substantial increase in central government revenue in the coming fiscal year. The new tax system also redefines income distribution and the power structure between the central and local governments. Finally, it propels China's further internationalization and its effort to catch up with world standards, because the concept behind it is borrowed from many advanced countries.[17] Such change will inevitably affect China's chance of entering the WTO (detailed in chapter 8).

Conceptual Change of Economic Planning

Planning is said to be a rational way of distributing a country's resources. In theory, it should be achievable and realistic. It has been a macro guiding principle for Chinese economic development since the first Five-Year Plan (1953–1957). The first plan was supposed to adapt China to the system of the former Soviet Union, but it was not wholeheartedly adopted by the Chinese. The second Five-Year Plan (1958–1962) and the third Five-Year Plan (1966–1970) were not implemented due to the chaos of the Great Leap Forward and the Cultural Revolution. Moreover, the objectives of the plans fell short because their socialist idealistic nature clashed with political power struggles happening in China.

After the cold war, the eighth Five-Year Plan (1991–1995) targeted economic development. In terms of sectoral growth, income distribution, control of the budget, and other social aspects, the plan clearly pointed toward market openness.[18] The major breakthrough came with the ninth Five-Year Plan (1996–2000), which outlines the structural transformation of a centrally planned economy into a market-oriented one.[19] Under this plan, "the enactment of a comprehensive and enforceable set of commercial laws and the growing size of the non-state sector should help define a more conducive business environment. All these would add vigor to the Chinese economy and help to maintain its future growth momentum."[20]

Prospects of China's Market Economy and U.S. Foreign Relations

Endogenous Changes to the Consumption Pattern

In the light of market forces, the exploration of how the consumption market affects the way of life of the people in the Southern part of China and those cities regarded as Special Economic Zones (SEZs) hinted at the directional change of the people's behavior.

The Tiananmen Incident in 1989 was a political outcry both to China or to the international community. However, the pace of marketization and the trend toward market economy in China were less affected. The 1992 Southern Tour of Deng Xiaoping, actually, shed light on the magnitude of the market economy and its openness in the coastal areas. In theory, the tour made by Deng Xiaoping consolidated policy favoring a market economy. In reality, the growth in Chinese domestic economy—for example, China's total exports in 1996 reached $151 billion[21]—caused a major concern for the world economy in relation to the creation of a "Greater China."[22] What concerns the international society is the feasibility of using economic development and market openness as the major locus of policy decision in China. To produce a comprehensive survey of the entire effect of market-oriented policy on China demands capacity beyond the scope of this book. Nevertheless, if we focus on the Quangdong province to illustrate the extent to which market-oriented policy changes consumption patterns, we might properly get a prior idea of how the society is being modified.

Apparently, the trend of the household purchase of durable goods from 1989 to 1995[23] demonstrated a general trend toward a "gentrification" of urban households. Thus, if we look more closely into the change of the profile, the addition of new items, and the structural change of the consumption pattern, more factors can be identified. First, the first fifteen items represent the core, or basic, necessities of measuring the living standard of urban household starting from 1989. Although the yearly change of the consumption of different items are roughly stable, some changes should be noticed. In the case of the purchase of sewing machines, a steady decrease was recorded. In 1989, 1.07 of sewing machine were purchased per 100 households (average). Yet in 1995, only 0.18 sewing machines were purchased per 100 households. In terms of percentages, it shows that there was an 83-percent reduction in the purchase of sewing machines. The reason behind this outcome is clearly due to an increase in the purchase of ready-made clothing from shops, instead of wearing hand-made garments. The market force, here, pulled the people from a self-reliant way of living into a modern society based on daily transactions and the division of labor.

More interestingly, beginning in 1994, the black-and-white television was no longer a unit of measurement of the standard of living in urban society. Neither did the automatic or electronic watch serve as a standard of measurement after 1992. Change of taste and the technological advancement changed the living standard of the people accordingly.

After 1992, the Chinese government added many new items to the list. These included a variety of goods, from furniture to electronic appliances. Apart from the increase in the standard of living, the wide use of electronic appliances hinted that the supply of electricity is more abundant. From the angle of social change, the use of range-hoods and ventilators could imply that people are living in multistoried apartment buildings, indicating that fewer and fewer people are living in houses and villages.

Among the newly added items, many were considered to be information- or knowledge-oriented. The installation of telephones and the use of pagers implied that communication and information will be more far-reaching. The increase in the effectiveness and the efficiency of the flow of information also affects the nurturing of a market economy in China. Whether we believe that information is a tool of government or an anti-government tool,[24] the power of knowledge and information[25] will generate a change based not just on the consumption patterns but also on individual behavior.

Change in behavior is clearly illustrated by a change in the consumption patterns of the people in Guangzhou. According to *Guangzhou Yearbook 1996,* two dramatic changes in consumption were indicated. First, the monthly demand for transportation and communication increased sharply from 24.41 yuen in 1994 to 39.69 yuen in 1995 per person, an increase of 62.60 percent.[26] Second, the monthly demand for merchandise and services also increased from 25.26 yuen in 1994 to 40.20 yuen in 1995 per person, 59.14 percent increase.[27] Due to the unique situation of Guangzhou, the change in consumption patterns might have outperformed many other provinces. Nevertheless, the structural change in the consumption pattern should not contradict that of the other provinces.

Exogenous Changes in U.S. Foreign Policy

Speaking to the Foreign Policy Association in January 1994, Jeffrey Garten, under secretary of commerce for international trade of the U.S. Commerce Department put forward the notion of promoting exports to the "big emerging markets (BEMs)."[28] Among ten BEMs, he identified China as the largest.[29] According to Garten, "the United States needs to give increased attention to supporting economic reforms that raise the standard of living in the BEMs."[30]

Sounding prophetic, Garten uses several chapters to further elaborate to the United States and even to the world what might occur, both positive and negative, if proper attitudes and policy orientations are undermined or neglected when dealing with BEMs. He contends that "certain big emerging markets are already part of this Western global framework, so the argument goes, then we should work more closely with them in order to deepen cooperation."[31]

In the post-cold war world economy, his idea of BEMs serves to educate the American public about the reality and changes of the world economy. Bearing the shrinking of U.S. power in mind, Garten basically attempts to remind Americans to be alert and prepared for the change and teach Americans how to work with other nations in the foreseeable future.

No sooner had he said this than U.S. secretary of commerce Ron Brown led a group of twenty-four businesspeople to China in August 1994. They were received by Wu Yi, the Chinese foreign trade minister. The trip was successful in that business contracts were eventually signed. For example, Michael Jordan and his Chinese counterparts signed fourteen agreements worth U.S.$140 million.[32]

On 4 May 1994, the Senate Subcommittee on East Asian and Pacific Affairs held a hearing entitled *U.S. Policy toward China*.[33] In general, the participants agreed upon the dismissal of a cold war strategy toward China.[34] In particular, as Robert Kapp, president of the U.S.-China Small Business Council, noted:

> Given the historical background I have discussed; given the immensity and the global importance of today's American encounter with China, and given the almost immeasurable challenges, dangers and opportunities that the United States and China must face in the future, we *must* (italics original) pursue full engagement for the long term with China.[35]

What type of policy will maximize benefits for the United States and China? The U.S. imports 18 percent of all of China's exports, estimated at U.S. $151 billion per year.[36] This implies that a policy based on market augmentation will help pinpoint their common interests in the years to come.

In addition, BEMs and U.S. foreign policy were further analyzed by Robert Chase, Emily Hill, and Paul Kennedy in a recent article which appeared in *Foreign Affairs* entitled: "Pivotal States and U.S. Strategy."[37] The objective of U.S. foreign policy toward these states is to "encourage integration of new security issues into a traditional, state-centered framework and lend greater clarity to the making of foreign policy."[38] On another occasion, when asked about U.S. policy toward China in relation to the concept of BEMs, Garten affirmatively replied "I think there's only one approach to China, and that is a policy of engagement, recognizing all the imperfections. The alternative, the so-called containment theory, to me is an insane approach."[39]

Finally, Deng Xiaoping, paramount leader, architect of China's economic reform and political hard-liner, died 19 February 1997.[40] His death had different meanings to different people. For those who participated in the 1989 democracy movement, it might be a juncture for reexamining the Tiananmen Incident and admitting that it was mishandled through military repression. For those who have benefited from economic openness, Deng's death will certainly force economic reform into a new battle between progressives and hard-liners.

In terms of Sino-American relations, many variables can affect both countries' perceptions of development and policy strategies. Hence, this book can, to a certain extent, serve as an alternative means of searching for the most possible points of convergence in Sino-American relations in the context of the market force. The tutelage of U.S. foreign policy and the establishment of market liberalization in China might be the first step towards China's recruitment into the world society.

Notes

1. Excerpted from a talk with United States envoy Brent Scowcroft on 10 December 1989. See Deng Xiaoping, *Selected Works of Deng Xiaoping, vol. 3*, (1982–1992) (Beijing: Foreign Languages Press, 1994): 338.
2. Cited in Peter Gourevitch, "The Second Image Reversed: The International Sources of Domestic Politics" *International Organization* 32, no. 4 (Autumn 1978): 885.
3. Susan Strange, *States and Markets*, 2d ed., (London: Pinter Publishers, 1994): 78.
4. *Constitution of the People's Republic of China* (Beijing: Foreign Languages Press, 1994): 94.
5. Ma Hung et al, eds., *What is Socialist Market Economy* (Beijing: Chinese Development Press, 1993).
6. Ibid., 3–16.
7. Ivan Tang, "Calls for Action on Industry 'Plague,'" *South China Morning Post*, 8 March 1997, 6.
8. Agatha Ngai and Daniel Kwan, "Jiang vow to Step Up State Sector Reforms" *South China Morning Post*, 4 March 1997, 10.
9. Agatha Ngai, "Shanghai Loses 290,000 jobs in Industrial Shift" *South China Morning Post*, 6 March 1997, 10.
10. *South China Morning Post*, 12 May 1997, 1 (Business section).
11. *Heng Seng Economic Monthly* (November 1992), 1.
12. Ibid, 3.
13. *Asian Monetary Monitor*, (May-June 1995): 14.
14. *People's Daily*, 15 November 1993, 1; *China News Analysis* (Taipei), 1 December 1993, 4 and *Wen Wei Po* (Hong Kong), 12 November 1993. For a more detailed explanation of the new tax system in late 1993, refer to the following three volumes: *Zhongguo gaige quenshu*, (1978–1991) (Dalian chubaishe, 1992), particularly the chapter called "Shuishou tizhi gaige juan"; Wang chuan lun and Wang ping wu (eds), *Zhongguo xinshuizhi yiwu quanshu* (Beijing: Zhongguo jingrong chubaishe, 1994) and Hao zhao cheng, et al., *Caishui: tizhi tupo yu liyi chongzu* (Beijing: Zhongguo caizheng jingji chubanshe, 1993). The first one gives a general historical perspective of the reforms after 1978 and criticisms of them, while the second concentrates on the late 1993 tax reform. The final book is one of a series concerning the structural change of Chinese economic development.
15. *Wen Wei Po* (Hong Kong), 16 November 1993.
16. *Daily Report*, China, FBIS-CHI-93-235, 9 December 1993, 24.
17. *China Economic News* 14, no. 48, 13 December 1993, 1–2 and *Beijing Review* 37, no.11, 14–20 March 1994, 12–15.

18. *China News Analysis*, 1 December 1995, 6.
19. *Hang Seng Economic Monthly*, November 1995, 1.
20. Ibid.
21. Seth Faison, "China Export Boom Also Benefits U.S.," *International Herald Tribune*, 5 March 1997, 1.
22. According to Harry Harding, the most common usage of "Greater China" refers to "the expansion of commercial ties among the three main Chinese economies [China, Hong Kong and Taiwan]." See Harry Harding, "The Concept of 'Greater China': Themes, Variations and Reservations" in *Greater China: The Next Superpower?* edited by David Shambaugh, (Oxford: Oxford University Press, 1995): 11.
23. See table 10.1 below:

TABLE 10.1
Urban Households' Purchase of Durable Goods, 1989–1995: An Average
(unit per 100 households)

Item	1989	1990	1991	1992	1993	1994	1995
Wardrobe	2.53	3.60	3.42	4.06	4.26	3.59	3.58
Desk	1.07	1.40	1.87	2.52	2.51	2.44	1.94
Bicycle	15.80	13.27	20.65	21.55	22.41	18.59	13.38
Sewing Machine	1.07	1.40	0.52	0.13	0.17	0.35	0.18
Clock	7.00	8.27	12.00	11.74	10.61	11.03	10.33
Electronic Fan	16.13	20.93	27.35	20.06	11.69	14.71	13.93
Washing Machine	3.80	3.20	3.03	3.29	5.65	3.86	3.61
Refrigerator	4.87	4.33	3.87	2.45	3.01	4.11	2.63
Radio	1.93	2.00	1.94	2.00	3.80	2.32	3.67
Color Television	4.87	2.93	3.87	4.58	3.83	6.71	5.44
Video Recorder	3.73	3.20	3.68	2.71	0.93	2.80	3.57
Camera	1.33	1.00	1.74	2.26	2.26	1.83	2.07
Black/White Television	1.20	0.33	0.32	0.39	0.36	—	—
Automatic Watch	6.33	7.33	6.71	—	—	—	—
Electronic Watch	5.27	11.00	10.58	—	—	—	—
Middle/High Class Musical Instruments	—	1.07	1.81	—	—	—	—
Electronic Cooker	—	6.33	10.65	7.23	7.95	9.97	8.84
Items appeared after 1992							
Assembled Furniture	—	—	—	1.81	2.46	3.00	2.34
Sofa-Bed	—	—	—	3.03	3.01	2.71	2.88
Sofa	—	—	—	12.71	11.54	8.15	11.36
Fan-Heater	—	—	—	0.39	0.64	0.17	0.14
Air-Conditioner	—	—	—	2.90	5.51	8.29	7.60
Electronic Cooker	—	—	—	7.23	7.95	9.97	8.84
Water Heater	—	—	—	5.42	6.10	7.90	5.74
Cooker-hood	—	—	—	5.61	5.76	5.34	4.03
Ventilator	—	—	—	2.71	2.15	2.45	2.91
Vacuum Cleaner	—	—	—	0.32	0.31	0.30	0.40
Motorcycle	—	—	—	1.81	3.32	3.26	2.93
Tricycle	—	—	—	0.39	0.26	0.36	0.32
Piano	—	—	—	0.26	0.05	0.13	—

Items related to information/knowledge and technology

Telephone	—	—	—	5.23	10.12	9.36	8.94
Pager	—	—	—	0.65	0.95	2.92	1.91
Electronic Game Machine	—	—	—	3.94	2.28	1.29	1.01
Hi-Fi System	—	—	—	1.29	2.81	3.30	2.70
Stereo Tape Recorder	—	—	—	0.90	1.81	1.26	1.34
Tape Recorder	—	—	—	3.68	2.29	3.72	3.20

Source: *Statistical Yearbook of Guangdong, 1990* (Beijing: China Statistical Publishing House, 1990): 450–451; *Statistical Yearbook of Guangdong, 1991* (Beijing: China Statistical Publishing House, 1991): 364; *Statistical Yearbook of Guangdong, 1992* (Beijing: China Statistical Publishing House, 1992): 407; *Statistical Yearbook of Guangdong, 1993* (Beijing: China Statistical Publishing House, 1993): 411; *Statistical Yearbook of Guangdong, 1994* (Beijing: China Statistical Publishing House, 1994): 366; *Statistical Yearbook of Guangdong, 1995* (Beijing: China Statistical Publishing House, 1995): 416; *Statistical Yearbook of Guangdong, 1996* (Beijing: China Statistical Publishing House, 1996): 414.

24. Joshua S. Goldstein, *International Relations* (New York: HarperCollins College Publishers, 1994): 411–416.
25. Peter F. Drucker, *Post-Capitalist Society* (New York: Harper Business, 1993): 183.
26. *Guangzhou Yearbook 1996* (Guangzhou: Guangzhou Yearbook Publisher, 1996): 383.
27. Ibid.
28. USIS, "U.S. Plans Trade Initiate Toward the Big Emerging Markets" *Economic Policy Backgrounder*, 26 January 1994, 1–18. The idea of BEMs was later published. See Jeffrey E. Garten, *The Big Ten: The Big Emerging Markets and How They Will Change Our Lives* (New York: Basic Books, 1997).
29. The ten markets are China, Indonesia, South Korea, India, Turkey, South Africa, Poland, Argentina, Brazil and Mexico. Ibid., USIS, 1.
30. Ibid.
31. Jeffrey E. Garten, *The Big Ten*, 65.
32. *South China Morning Post*, 30 August 1994.
33. U.S. Senate Committee on Foreign Relations, *U.S. Policy toward China: Hearing before the Subcommittee on East Asian and Pacific Affairs*, 103d Cong., 2d sess., 4 May 1994.
34. Ibid., 33.
35. Ibid., 75.
36. Steven Mufson, "U.S. Trade Debate is Crucial to China's Growth" *International Herald Tribune*, 2 May 1997, 19.
37. Robert Chase, Emily Hill, and Paul Kennedy, "Pivotal States and U.S. Strategy" *Foreign Affairs Agenda, 1996* (New York: Foreign Affairs, 1996): 44–59.
38. Ibid., 47.
39. Jeffrey E. Garten is currently the dean of the Yale School of Management and former U.S. undersecretary of commerce for international trade. He made this statement when he was interviewed by Brian Knowlton. See *International Herald Tribune*, 11 June 1997.
40. Although Deng Xiaoping died at 21:08, the official announcement was made by Xinhua at 2:41 on 20 February 1997. *South China Morning Post*, 20 February 1997, 1 and *Wen Wei Po*, 20 February 1997, 1.

Appendix

Chronology of Sino-U.S. Relations after 1972

1972 21–28 February. U.S. President Richard Nixon visits China, issues the Shanghai Communiqué and opens the door to renewed Sino-U.S. relations.

1973 22 February. China and the United States announce the establishment of Liaison Offices in each other's capitals.

1975 1–5 December. U.S. President Gerald Ford visits China.

1978 16 December. China and the United States simultaneously publish a joint communiqué on the establishment of diplomatic relations.

1979 1 January. China and the United States formally establish diplomatic relations.

28 January. Chinese Vice Premier Deng Xiaoping officially visits the United States.

10 April. U.S. President Jimmy Carter signs the "Taiwan Relations Act."

31 December. The United States ends its "joint defense treaty" with Taiwan signed in 1954.

1982 17 August. China and the United States sign the communiqué of 17 August in which the United States pledges to reduce its arms sales to Taiwan.

1984 25 April–1 May. U.S. President Ronald Reagan visits China.

1985 22 July–2 August. Chinese President Li Xiannian visits the United States.

1987 17 October. China condemns the U.S. Senate for interfering in China's internal affairs by passing a bill on the so-called "Tibetan issue."

1989 25–26 February. U.S. President George Bush pays a working visit to China.

25 May. The United States lists China as a country under the "super 301" article.

29 June and 4 July. The U.S. House of Representatives and Senate respectively adopt a resolution imposing sanctions on China.

1990 22 February. China protests the U.S. State Department "human rights report" for severely encroaching on China's sovereignty.

24 May. U.S. President George Bush decides to renew the MFN trade status to China for another year.

1992 17 January. China and the United States reach a Memorandum of Understanding on Protecting Intellectual Property Rights.
30 January. Chinese Premier Li Peng meets with U.S. President Bush at UN Headquarters.
18 June. China and the United States reach a Memorandum of Understanding on Forbidding Import and Export of Prison Labor Products.
6–10 October. China and the United States reach a Memorandum of Understanding on Market Access.

1993 19 November. Chinese President Jiang Zemin meets with U.S. President Bill Clinton at the informal summit of the Asia-Pacific Economic Cooperation in Seattle.

1994 11–14 March. U.S. Secretary of State Warren Christopher visits China.
2 May. U.S. President Clinton announces a decoupling of China's MFN status from its human rights record.
16–19 October. U.S. Secretary of Defense William Perry visits China.
14 November. President Jiang Zemin meets with U.S. President Clinton for the second time at the informal summit of Asia-Pacific Economic Cooperation in Jakarta.
31 December. The United States puts Chinese products worth U.S. $2.8 billion onto a list of temporary sanctions for alleged China's "infringement" upon U.S. intellectual property rights.

1995 17–28 January. Sino-U.S. negotiations on intellectual property rights are held in Beijing without reaching an agreement.
11 March. China and the United States sign an agreement on intellectual property rights.
22 May. The U.S. government grants U.S. visa to President Lee Tenghui of Taiwan.
24 October. President Jiang holds talks with President Clinton in New York.

1996 6 July. Assistant to the U.S. President for Security Affairs Anthony Lake visits China to pave the way for high-level visits.

1997 28 March. Newt Gingrich visits China.
26 March. U.S. Vice-President Al Gore visits China.
April. U.S. Secretary of State Madeleine Albright visits China.
26 October–3 November. President Jiang Zemin of China visits the United States.

1998 17–19 January. U.S. Defense Secretary William Cohen visits China.

Bibliography

Ambrose, Stephen E. 1993. *Rise to Globalism: American Foreign Policy Since 1938*. 2d ed. London: Penguin Books.

American Friends Service Committee. 1965. *A New China Policy: Some Quaker Proposals*. New Haven: Yale University Press.

Asia and the World Forum. 1977. *Forum on the U.S. and East Asia*. Monograph Series, no. 7. Taipei: Asia and the World Forum.

Asian Wall Street Journal. Various issues.

Baldwin, David A. 1993. *Key Concepts in International Political Economy, vols. 1 and 2*. Hants: Edward Elgar Publishing Limited.

Barnett, A. Doak. 1977. *China and the Major Powers in East Asia*. Washington, DC: Brookings Institution.

Bernstein, Richard and Ross H. Munro. 1997. *The Coming Conflict with China*. New York: Alfred A. Knopf.

Briggs, Philip J. 1981. "Congress and the Cold War: U.S-China Policy, 1955." *China Quarterly*, no. 85 (March): 80–95.

Brinkley, Douglas. 1997. "Democratic Enlargement: The Clinton Doctrine." *Foreign Policy*, no. 106 (Spring): 111–127.

Brown, Lester R. 1995. *Who Will Feed China? Wake-Up Call for a Small Planet*. New York: W. W. Norton and Company.

Brown, Seyom. 1994. *The Faces of Power: Constancy and Change in United States Foreign Policy from Truman to Clinton*, 2d ed. New York: Columbia University Press.

Burnell, Elaine H. 1969. *Asian Dilemma: United States, Japan and China*. California: The Center for the Study of Democratic Institutions.

Bush, George. 1992. *U.S. Policy in the Asia-Pacific Region: Meeting the Challenges of the Post Cold-War Era*. Singapore Lecture 1992. Singapore: Institute of Southeast Asian Studies.

Cai, Wenguo. 1992."China's GATT Membership: Selected Legal and Political Issues." *Journal of World Trade* 26, no. 1 (February); 35–61.

Campbell, David. 1992. *Writing Security: United States Foreign Policy and the Politics of Identity*. Minneapolis: University of Minnesota Press.

Caporaso, James A. and David P. Levine. 1992. *Theories of Political Economy*. Cambridge: Cambridge University Press.

Carr, E. H. [1939]1995. *The Twenty Years' Crisis 1919–1939*. London: Macmillan, Papermac.

Center for Strategic and International Studies. 1992 *Hong Kong in the MFN Debate: CSIS Project on Democracy, Prosperity, and Stability in the Future of Hong Kong and East Asia.* Washington, DC: The Center for Strategic and International Studies.

Chan, Steve. 1993. *East Asian Dynamism: Growth, Order, and Security in the Pacific Region.* 2d ed. Boulder, CO: Westview Press.

Chandler, Alfred D., Jr. 1990. *Scale and Scope: The Dynamics of Industrial Capitalism.* Cambridge, MA: Harvard University Press, The Belknap Press.

Chew, Ernest C. T. and Edwin Lee. 1991. *A History of Singapore.* Singapore: Oxford University Press.

China White Paper, The. 1967. vols. 1 and 2. Stanford, CA: Stanford University Press.

Cohen, Jerome Alan, Robert F. Dernberger and John R. Garson. 1971. *China Trade Prospects and U.S. Policy.* New York: Praeger Publishers.

Cohen, Warren I. 1996. *Pacific Passage.* New York: Columbia University Press.

Congressional Quarterly Service. 1967. *China and U. S. Far East Policy 1945–1967.* Washington, DC: Congressional Quarterly Service.

Copper, John F. 1992. *China Diplomacy: The Washington-Taipei-Beijing Triangle.* Boulder, CO: Westview Press.

Cox, Michael. 1995. *U.S. Foreign Policy after the Cold War: Superpower without a Mission?* London: Pinter, Royal Institute of International Affairs.

Crane, George T. and Abla M. Amawi, eds. 1991. *The Theoretical Evolution of International Political Economy: A Reader.* New York: Oxford Univeristy Press.

Cumings Bruce. 1984. "The Origins and Development of the Northeast Asian Political Economy: Industrial Sectors, Product Cycles, and Political Consequences." *International Organization* 38, no.1 (Winter): 1–40.

———. 1996. "The World Shakes China." *The National Interest*, no. 43 (Spring): 28–41.

Deng, Mao Mao. 1995. *My Father Deng Xiaoping.* Translated by Lin Xiangming and others. New York: BasicBooks.

Deng, Xiaoping. 1993. *Deng Xiaoping Wenxuan, vol. 3.* Beijing: Renmin Chubaishe.

———. 1994. *Deng Xiaoping Wenxuan, vol. 1.* Beijing: Renmin Chubaishe.

———. 1994. *Deng Xiaoping Wenxuan, vol. 2.* Beijing: Renmin Chubaishe.

Domes, Jurgen. 1990. *After Tiananmen Square: Challenges for the Chinese-American Relationship.* Cambridge, MA: Institute for Foreign Policy Analysis, Inc.

Downen, Robert L. 1981. *Of Grave Concern, U.S.-Taiwan Relations on the Threshold of the 1980s.* Significant Issues Series, vol. 3, no. 4. Washington, DC: The Center for Strategic and International Studies, Georgetown University.

Drucker, Peter F. 1968. *The Age of Discontinuity*. New York: Harper and Row.

———. 1990. *The New Realities*. London: Mandarin.

———. 1993. *Post-Capitalist Society*. New York: Harper Business.

———. 1993. *The Ecological Vision: Reflections on the American Condition*. New Brunswick, NJ: Transaction Publishers.

———. 1994. "The Theory of the Business," *Harvard Business Review* 72, no. 5 (September-October): 95–104.

Dulles, Foster Rhea. 1972. *American Foreign Policy Toward Communist China 1949–1969*. New York: Thomas Y. Crowell Company.

Economist, The. Various issues.

Elster, Jon. "Rationality, Emotions, and Social Norms." *Synthese* 98 (1994): 21–49.

Fairbank, John King. *The United States and China*. 4th ed. enlarged. Cambridge, MA: Harvard University Press, 1983.

Fallows, James. 1995. *Looking at the Sun: The Rise of the New East Asian Economic and Political System*. New York: Vintage Books.

Feintech, Lynn Diane. 1981. *China's Four Modernizations and the United States*. Headline Series 255. New York: Foreign Policy Association.

Foot, Rosemary. 1995. *The Practice of Power: U.S. Relations with China Since 1949*. Oxford: Clarendon Press.

Frank, Andre Gunder. 1970. *Latin America: Underdevelopment or Revolution*. New York: Monthly Review Press.

Frey, Bruno S. 1984. *International Political Economics*. Oxford: Basil Blackwell.

Friedberg, Aaron L. 1994."The Future of American Power." *Political Science Quarterly* 109, no. 1: 1–22.

Frieden, Jeffrey A. and David A. Lake, eds. 1991. *International Political Economy: Perspectives on Global Power and Wealth*. 2d ed. London: Unwin Hyman.

Friedman, Edward. 1996. "Why China Matters." *Journal of International Affairs* 49, no. 2 (Winter): 302–308.

Friedman, Edward and Mark Selden, eds. 1971. *America's Asia: Dissenting Essays on Asian-American Relations*. New York: Vintage Books.

Fukuyama, Francis. 1992. *The End of History and the Last Man*. New York: Avon Books.

———. 1995. *Trust: The Social Virtues and the Creation of Prosperity*. New York: The Free Press.

Gao, Mobo C. F. 1992. "Democracy, What Democracy? China's Road to Modernization." *China Report* 28, no. 1: 13–25.

Garson, Robert. 1994. *The United States and China Since 1949: A Troubled Affair*. London: Pinter Publishers.

Garten, Jeffrey E. 1997. *The Big Ten: The Big Emerging Markets and How They Will Change Our Lives*. New York: BasicBooks.

Garver, John W. 1980. "Chinese Foreign Policy in 1970: The Tilt Towards the Soviet Union." *The China Quarterly*, no. 82 (June): 241–249.

———. 1982. *China's Decision for Rapprochement with the United States, 1968–1971*. Boulder, CO: Westview Press.

———. 1993. *Foreign Relations of the People's Republic of China*. Englewood Cliffs, NJ: Prentice-Hall.

Gill, Stephen R. 1993. "Neo-Liberalism and the Shift Towards a US-Centerd Transnational Hegemony." In Overbeek and Henk, *Restructuring Hegemony in the Global Political Economy: The Rise of Transnational Neo-Liberalism in the 1980s*, pp. 246–282. London: Routledge.

Gilpin, Robert. 1987. *The Political Economy of International Relations*. Princeton, NJ: Princeton University Press.

Gold, Thomas B. 1986. *State and Society in the Taiwan Miracle*. New York: M. E. Sharpe, Inc., 1986.

Goodnight, Lynn, James Hunter, and Eric Truett, eds. 1995. *Changing the Policy of the United States Government Toward the People's Republic of China*. Lincolnwood, IL: National Textbook Company.

Gordon, Bernard K. 1990. *New Directions for American Policy in Asia*. London: Routledge.

———. 1990–91."The Asian-Pacific Rim: Success at a Price." *Foreign Affairs* 70, no.1: 142–159.

Haass, Richard N. 1995. "Paradigm Lost." *Foreign Affairs* 74, no. 1 (January/February): 43–58.

Haggard, Stephan. 1990. *Pathways from the Periphery: The Politics of Growth in the Newly Industrializing Countries*. Ithaca, NY: Cornell University Press.

——— and Beth A. Simmons. 1987. "Theories of International Regimes." *International Organization* 41, no.3. (Summer): 491–517.

Harding, Harry, ed. 1984. *China's Foreign Relations in the 1980s*. New Haven, CT: Yale University Press.

———. 1992. *A Fragile Relationship: the United States and China Since 1972*. Washington, DC: The Brookings Institution.

Harland, Bryce. 1996. *Collision Course: America and East Asia in the Past and the Future*. Singapore: Institute of Southeast Asian Studies.

Harlow, Robert John. 1965. "United States Problems in Eastern Asia and the Role of the Seventh Fleet." Master's thesis. The American University, Washington, DC.

Hayek, Friedrich A. 1944. *The Road to Serfdom*. Chicago: The University of Chicago Press.

Hebei Ribao. Various issues.

Hendrickson, David C. 1994. "The Recovery of Internationalism." *Foreign Affairs* 73, no.5. (September/October): 26–43.

Hicks, John D. 1949. *A Short History of American Democracy*. Boston, MA: Houghton Mifflin.

Hilsman, Roger. 1964. *To Move a Nation.* New York: Delta Books.

Hinton, Harold C., ed. 1982. *Government and Politics in Revolutionary China: Selected Documents, 1949–1979.* Wilmington, DE: Scholarly Resources Inc.

Hong Kong Economic Journal. Various issues.

Honolulu Advertiser, The. Various issues.

Hornik, Richard. 1994. "Bursting China's Bubble." *Foreign Affairs* 73, no. 3 (May/June): 28–42.

Huntington, Samuel P. 1993."The Clash of Civilization?" *Foreign Affairs* 72, no. 3 (Summer): 22–49.

———. 1996. *The Clash of Civilizations and the Remaking of World Order.* New York: Simon and Schuster.

———. 1996."The West: Unique, Not Universal." *Foreign Affairs* 75, no. 6 (November/December): 28–46.

Inoguchi, Takashi and Daniel I. Okimoto, eds. 1988. *The Political Economy of Japan: The Changing International Context, vol. 2.* Stanford, CA: Stanford University Press.

International Herald Tribune. Various issues.

Isaak, Robert A. 1991. *International Political Economy: Managing World Economic Change.* Englewood Cliffs, NJ: Prentice-Hall, Inc.

Jacobson, Harold K. and Michel Oksenberg. 1990. *China's Participation in the IMF, the World Bank, and GATT: Toward a Global Economic Order.* Ann Arbor, MI: The University of Michigan Press.

Jiang, Arnold Xiangze. 1988. *The United States and China.* Chicago, IL: The University of Chicago Press.

Johnson, Chalmers. 1996. "Containing China: U.S. and Japan Drift Toward Disaster." *Japan Quarterly* 43, no. 4 (October-December): 10–18.

——— and E. B. Keehn. 1995. "The Pentagon's Ossified Strategy." *Foreign Affairs* 74, no. 4 (July/August): 103–114.

Jordan, Amos Azariah, Jr. 1961. "Foreign Aid and Defense: United States Military and Related Economic Assistance to Southeast Asia." Ph.D. diss., Columbia University.

Kang, T. W. 1989. *Is Korea the Next Japan? Understanding the Structure, Strategy, and Tactics of America's Next Competitor.* New York: The Free Press.

Kennan, George F. ("By X"). 1947. "The Sources of Soviet Conduct." *Foreign Affairs* 25, no. 4 (July): 566–582.

———. 1951. *American Diplomacy 1900–1950.* New York: New American Library.

———. 1993. *Around the Cragged Hill: A Personal and Political Philosophy.* New York: W. W. Norton and Company.

———. 1995. "On American Principles." *Foreign Affairs* 74, no. 2 (March/April): 116–126.

Kennedy, Paul. 1989. *The Rise and Fall of The Great Powers: Economic Change and Military Conflict from 1500 to 2000.* London: Fontana Press.

Keohane, Robert O. 1984."The Political Economy and the Crisis of Embedded Liberalism." In John H. Goldthorpe, ed. *Order and Conflict in Contemporary Capitalism*. New York: Oxford University Press.

———. 1984. *After Hegemony: Cooperation and Discord in the World Political Economy*. Princeton, NJ: Princeton University Press.

Keohane, Robert O. and Joseph S. Nye. 1989. *Power and Interdependence*. 2d ed. New York: Harper Collins Publishers.

Kindleberger, Charles P. 1981. "Dominance and Leadership in the International Economy: Exploitation, Public Goods, and Free Rides." *International Studies Quarterly* 25, no.2. (June): 242–254.

Lampton, David M. 1974. "Health Policy During the Great Leap Forward" *The China Quarterly*, no. 60 (October/ December): 668–698.

Lardy, Nicholas R. 1987. *China's Entry into the World Economy: Implications for Northeast Asia and the United States*. London: University Press of America.

Lasater, Martin L. 1962. *The Security of Taiwan: Unraveling the Dilemma,* vol. 4, no. 1, *Significant Issues Series*. Washington, DC: The Center for Strategic and International Studies Georgetown University.

Latourette, Kenneth Scott. 1946. *The United States Moves Across The Pacific*. New York: Harper and Brothers.

Ling, L. H. M. 1996. "Hegemony and the Internationalizing State: A Post-Colonial Analysis of China's Integration into Asian Corporatism." *Review of International Political Economy* 3, no. 1 (Spring): 1–26.

Liu, Shia-Ling. 1988. *U.S. Foreign Policy toward Communist China in the 1970s: The Misadventures of Presidents Nixon, Ford and Carter*. Taipei: Kuang Lu Publishing Co.

Ma, Hung et al., eds. 1993. *What is Socialist Market Economy?* Beijing: Chinese Development Press.

Mandelbaum, Michael, ed. 1995. *The Strategic Quadrangle: Russia, China, Japan, and the United States in East Asia*. New York: Council on Foreign Relations Press.

Mao, Tse-Tung. 1967. *Selected Works of Mao Zedong, vol. 2*. Peking: Foreign Languages Press.

———. 1977. *Selected Works of Mao Zedong, vol. 5*. Peking: Foreign Languages Press.

McCormick, Thomas J. 1970. *China Market: America's Quest for Informal Empire 1893–1901*. Chicago: Quadrangle Paperbacks.

———. 1995. *America's Half-Century: United States Foreign Policy in the Cold War and After*. 2d ed. Baltimore, MD: The Johns Hopkins University Press.

McNamara, Robert S. 1989. *Out of the Cold: New Thinking for American Foreign and Defense Policy in the Twenty-First Century*. New York: Simon and Schuster.

Milner, Helen. 1993. "Maintaining International Commitments in Trade Policy." In R. Kent Weaver and Bert A. Rockman, eds. *Do Institutions Matter?: Government Capabilities in the United States and Abroad*. Washington, DC: The Brookings Institution.

Moon, Chung-In. 1990. "The Future of the Newly Industrialising Countries: An 'Uncertain Promise'?" In Dennis C. Pirages and Christine Sylvester, eds. *Transformations in the Global Political Economy*, pp. 153–194. London: Macmillan.

Nash, Henry T. 1973. *American Foreign Policy: Response to a Sense of Threat*. Homewood, IL: The Dorsey Press.

Nathan, Andrew J. 1993. "China's Path from Communism." *Journal of Democracy* 4, no. 2 (April): 37–39.

Nathan, Andrew J. and Robert S. Ross. 1997. *The Great Wall and the Empty Fortress: China's Search for Security*. New York: W. W. Norton and Company.

Newson, David D. 1988. *Diplomacy and the American Democracy*. Bloomington, IN: Indiana University Press.

Nixon, Richard. 1978. *RN: The Memoirs of Richard Nixon*. London: Sidgwick and Jackson.

North, D. 1990. *Institutions, Institutional Change and Economic Performance*. Cambridge: Cambridge University Press.

Nye, Joseph S. 1990. *Bound to Lead: The Changing Nature of American Power*. New York: Basic Books.

———. 1993. *Understanding International Conflicts: An Introduction to Theory and History*. New York: HarperCollins College Publishers.

———. 1995. "The Case for Deep Engagement." *Foreign Affairs* 74, no. 4 (July/August): 90–102.

Nye, Joseph and Robert O. Keohane. 1971. "Transnational Relations and World Politics: An Introduction." *International Organization* 25: 329–349.

Ohmae, Kenichi. 1993. "The Rise of The Region State." *Foreign Affairs* 72, no.2 (Spring): 78–87.

———. 1995. *The End of The Nation State: The Rise of Regional Economies*. New York: The Free Press.

Olson, Mancur. 1982. *The Rise and Decline of Nations*. New Haven, CT: Yale University Press.

———. 1993. "Dictatorship, Democracy, and Development." *American Political Science Review* 87, no.3 (September): 567–576.

Overholt, William H. 1993. *The Rise of China: How Economic Reform is Creating a New Superpower*. New York: W. W. Norton and Company.

Palmer, Norman D. 1991. *The New Regionalism in Asia and the Pacific*. Mass: Lexington Books.

Pearson, Margaret. 1991. *Joint Ventures in the People's Republic of China*. Princeton, NJ: Princeton University Press.

Pollack, Jonathan D. 1984. *The Lessons of Coalition Politics: Sino-American Security Relations*. A Project Air Force Report Prepared for the United States Air Force. Rand Corporation.

Popper, Karl. 1995. *The Open Society and Its Enemies*. Golden Jubilee Edition. London: Routledge.

Przeworski, Adam. 1991. *Democracy and the Market: Political and Economic Reforms in Eastern Europe and Latin America*. New York: Cambridge University Press.

Putnam, Robert D. 1995. "Bowing Alone: America's Declining Social Capital." *Journal of Democracy* 6, no. 1 (January): 65–78.

Reich, Robert B. 1992. *The Work of Nations: Preparing Ourselves for Twenty-first-Century Capitalism*. New York: Vintage Books.

Renmin Ribio. Various issues.

Rhee, Jong-Chan. 1994. *The State and Industry in South Korea: The Limits of the Authoritarian State*. London: Routledge.

Richman, Barry M. 1969. *Industrial Society in Communist China*. New York: Vintage Books.

Rielly, John E., ed. 1987. *American Public Opinion and U.S. Foreign Policy 1987*. Chicago: The Chicago Council on Foreign Relations.

Riskin, Carl. 1987. *China's Political Economy: The Quest for Development Since 1949*. New York: Oxford University Press.

Robinson, Thomas W. and David Shambaugh, ed. 1994. *Chinese Foreign Policy: Theory and Practice*. Oxford: Clarendon Press.

Ross, Robert. 1996. "Enter the Dragon." *Foreign Policy*, no. 104 (Fall): 18–25.

Rostow, W. W. 1990. *The Stages of Economic Growth: A Non-communist Manifesto*. 3d ed. New York: Cambridge University Press.

Rowland, Robert C. 1995. *United States Policy Toward the People's Republic of China: An Overview of the Issues*. Lincolnwood, IL: National Textbook Company.

Rusk, Dean. 1963. *The Winds of Freedom*. Boston, MA: Beacon Press.

Segal, Gerald. 1994."China's Changing Shape." *Foreign Affairs* 73, no. 3 (May/June): 43–58.

Shambaugh, David., ed. 1995. *Greater China: The Next Superpower?* Oxford: Oxford University Press.

———. 1996."Containment or Engagement of China?" *International Security* 21, no. 2 (Fall): 180–209.

Shirk, Susan L. 1993.*The Political Logic of Economic Reform in China*. Berkeley: University of California Press.

Snow, Edgar. 1973. *Red Star Over China*. Revised and Enlarged. New York: Grove Press.

South China Morning Post. Various issues.

Sichuan Ribao. Various issues.

Spanier, John W. 1968. *American Foreign Policy Since World War II*. 3d rev. ed. New York: Frederick A. Praeger.

Spero, Joan Edelman. 1990. *The Politics of International Economic Relations*. 4th ed. London: Routledge.

Stiles, Kendall W and Akaha Tsuneo, eds. 1991. *International Political Economy: A Reader*: New York: HarperCollins Publishers.

Stoessinger, John G. 1994. *Nations at Dawn: China, Russia and America*, 6th ed. New York: McGraw-Hill, Inc.

Strange, Susan. 1994. *States and Markets*. 2d. ed. London: Pinter Publishers.

Stubbs, Richard. 1994. "The Political Economy of the Asia-Pacific Region" In *Political Economy and the Changing Global Order*. Edited by R. Stubbs, Richard and Geoffrey R. D. Underhill, pp. 366–377. London: Macmillan.

Sun, Yan. 1995. *The Chinese Reassessment of Socialism, 1976–1992*. Princeton, NJ: Princeton University Press.

Sutter, Robert G. 1992. *East Asia and the Pacific: Challenge for U.S. Policy*. Boulder:, CO: Westview Press.

Sylvester, Christine. 1990. "The Emperors' Theories and Transformations: Looking at the Field through Feminist Lenses." In Dennis C. Pirages and Christine Sylvester, eds. *Transformation in the Global Political Economy*, pp. 230–253. London: Macmillan.

Ta Kung Pao, Weekly Supplement.

Thucydides. [c. 411 B.C.]1972. *History of the Peloponnesian War*. Translated by Rex Warner. London: Penguin Books.

Tsou, Tang. 1963. *America's Failure in China 1941–50*. Chicago: The University of Chicago Press.

Toffler, Alvin. 1991. *Power Shift: Knowledge, Wealth, and Violence at the Edge of the Twenty-first Century*. New York: Bantam Books.

U.S. House. 1971. Committee on Foreign Affairs. *United States-Republic of China Relations: Hearings before the Subcommittee on Asian and Pacific Affairs*. 92nd Cong., 1st sess., 20, 21 and 26 October.

U.S. House. 1971. Committee on Foreign Affairs. *Newsman's Visit to China: Briefing by William Attwood, Publisher of NEWSDAY: Hearing before the Subcommittee on Asian and Pacific Affairs*. 92nd Cong., 1st sess., 3 November.

U.S. House. 1972. Committee on Foreign Affairs. *The New China Policy: Its Impact on the United States and Asia: Hearings before the Subcommittee on Asian and Pacific Affairs*. 92nd Cong., 2nd sess., 2, 3, 4, 16, and 17 May.

U.S. House. 1979. Committee on Foreign Affairs. Subcommittee on Foreign Affairs. *China and Asia-An Analysis of China's Recent Policy Toward Neighboring States*. Report by the Foreign Affairs and National Defense Division, Congressional Research Service, Library of Congress, Preceded by a State Department Report on Normalization Negotiations With China. 96th Cong., 1st sess., March. Committee Print.

U.S. House. 1979. Committee on Foreign Affairs. Subcommittee on Asian and Pacific Affairs. *Recognizing the People's Republic of China: The Experience of Japan, Australia, France and West Germany.* Report prepared by the Foreign Affairs and National Defense Division, Congressional Research Service, Library of Congress. 96th Cong., 1st sess., May. Committee Print.

U.S. House. 1979. Committee on Foreign Affairs. Subcommittee on Asian and Pacific Affairs. *Playing the China Card: Implications for United States-Soviet-Chinese Relations.* Report prepared by the Foreign Affairs and National Defense Division, Congressional Research Service, Library of Congress. 96th Cong., October. Committee Print.

U.S. House. 1980. Committee on Foreign Affairs. *China Claims Reallocation: Hearing and Markup before the Committee on Foreign Affairs and its Subcommittee on Asian and Pacific Affairs.* 96th Cong., 2nd sess., 29 and 30 September.

U.S. House. 1982. Committee on Ways and Means. *Extension of MFN Status to Romania, Hungary, and the People's Republic of China: Hearings before the Subcommittee on Trade.* 97th Cong., 2nd sess., 12 and 13 July.

U.S. House. 1984. Committee on Foreign Affairs. *United States-China Relations: Hearings Before the Committee on Foreign Affairs and its Subcommittee on Asian and Pacific Affairs.* 98th Cong., 2nd sess., 3 and 4 April and 5 June.

U.S. House. 1987. Committee on Foreign Affairs. *Development in United States-Japan Economic Relations, May 1987: Hearings Before the Subcommittees on Asian and Pacific Affairs.* 100th Cong., 23 April and 5 May.

U.S. House. 1987. Committee on Foreign Affairs. *Developments in China, February 1987: Hearing before the Subcommittee on Asian and Pacific Affairs.* 100th Cong., 1st sess., 5 February.

U.S. House. 1989. Committee on Foreign Affairs. *The Wave of Protest in the People's Republic of China: Hearing before the Subcommittee on Asian and Pacific Affairs.* 101st Cong., 1st sess., 4 May.

U.S. House. 1990. Committee on Foreign Affairs. *United States Policy Toward China: Hearing before the Committee on Foreign Affairs.* 101st Cong., 2nd sess., 8 February.

U.S. House. 1990. Committee on Foreign Affairs. *Most-Favored-Nation Status for the People's Republic of China: Hearings before the Subcommittee on Human Rights and International Organizations, Asian and Pacific Affairs, and on International Economic Policy and Trade.* 101st Cong., 2nd sess., 16 and 24 May.

U.S. House. 1991. Committee on Foreign Affairs. *Most Favored Nation Status for the People's Republic of China: Joint Hearing before the Subcommittee on Human Rights and International Organization; Asian and Pacific*

Affairs and International Economic Policy and Trade. 102d Cong., 1st sess., 29 May.

U.S. House. 1991. Committee on Foreign Affairs. *Renewal of MFN Trading Status for the People's Republic of China: Hearing and Markup before the Committee on Foreign Affairs.* 102d Cong., 1st sess., on H. Con. Res. 174. 26 June.

U.S. House. 1991. Committee on Foreign Affairs. *Chinese Forced Labor Exports to The United States: Hearing before the Subcommittees on Human Rights and International Organizations and on International Economic Policy and Trade.* 102nd Cong., 1st sess., 23 Sept. and 5 Dec.

U.S. House. 1993. Committee on Foreign Affairs. *U.S. Foreign Policy in the Post-Cold War Era.* Report and Recommendations by Hon. Lee H. Hamilton, Chairman. 103rd Cong., 1st sess., May. Committee Print.

U.S. House. 1993. Committee on Foreign Affairs. *Chinese Forced Labor Exports to the United States: Joint Hearing before the Subcommittees on Economic Policy, Trade and Environment; International Security, International Organizations and Human Rights; and Asia and the Pacific.* 103d Cong., 1st sess., 9 September.

U.S. House. 1994. Committee on Foreign Affairs. *China: Human Rights and MFN: Joint Hearing before the Subcommittees on Economic Policy, Trade and Environment; International Security, International Organizations and Human Rights; and Asia and the Pacific.* 103d Cong., 2d sess., 24 March.

U.S. House. 1994. Committee on Foreign Affairs. *Should Taiwan be Admitted to the United Nation?: Joint Hearing before the Subcommittees on International Security, International Organizations and Human Rights and Asia and the Pacific.* 103d Cong., 2nd sess., 14 July.

United State Information Service (USIS). *Foreign Policy Backgrounder.* Various issues.

U.S. Joint Economic Committee Congress of the United States. 1967. *The Future of U.S. Foreign Trade Policy: Hearings before the Subcommittee on Foreign Economic Policy.* 90th Cong., 1st sess., 11, 12, 13, 18, 19 and 29 July.

United States Relations with China: With Special Reference to the Period 1944-1949. 1968. New York: Greenwood Press.

U. S. Senate. 1959. Committee on Foreign Relations. *United States Foreign Policy: ASIA.* 86th Cong., 1st sess., 1 November. Committee Print.

U.S. Senate. 1962. Committee on the Judiciary. *Refugee Problem in Hong Kong and Macao: Hearings before the Subcommittee to Investigate Problems Connected with Refugees and Escapees.* 87th Cong., 2d sess., 29 May; 7, 8, 28 June; and 10 July.

U.S. Senate. 1970. Committee on Foreign Relations. *United States Security Agreements and Commitments Abroad Republic of Korea: Hearings Be-*

fore the Subcommittee on United States Security Agreements and Commitments Abroad. 91th Cong., 2d sess., 24, 25 and 26 February.

U.S. Senate. 1970. Committee on the Judiciary. Subcommittee to Investigate the Administration of the Internal Security Act and other Internal Security Laws. *The Amerasia papers: A Clue to the Catastrophe of China,* vols. 1 and 2. 91th Cong., 1st sess., 26 January. Committee Print.

U.S. Senate. 1982. Committee on Agriculture, Nutrition, and Forestry. *Proposed Eligibility of The People's Republic of China for Participation in the Food for Peace Program: Hearings before the Committee on Agriculture, Nutrition, and Forestry.* 97th Cong., 2d sess., 3 May.

U.S. Senate. 1982. Committee on the Judiciary. *Taiwan Communiqué and Separation of Powers: Hearings before the Subcommittee on Separation of Powers.* 97th Cong., 2d sess., 17 and 27.

U.S. Senate. 1983. Committee on the Judiciary. *Taiwan Communiqué and Separation of Powers: Hearing before the Subcommittee on Separation of Powers.* 98th Cong., 1st sess., 10 March.

U.S. Senate. 1990. Committee on Foreign Relations. *Sino-American Relations: One Year After the Massacre at Tiananmen Square: Hearing before the Subcommittee on East Asian and Pacific Affairs.* 101st Cong., 2nd sess., 6 June.

U.S. Senate Committee on Foreign Relations. *U.S. Policy Toward China: Hearing before the Subcommittee on East Asian and Pacific Affairs.* 103rd Cong., 2nd sess., 4 May 1994.

Vogel, Ezra F. 1991. *The Four Little Dragons: The Spread of Industrialization in East Asia.* Cambridge, MA: Harvard University Press.

Wallop, Malcolm. 1993. "America Needs a Post-Containment Doctrine." *Orbis* (Spring): 187–203.

Wanamaker, Temple. 1969. *American Foreign Policy Today.* New York: Bantam Books.

Wang, Guiguo. 1994. "China's Return to GATT: Legal and Economic Implications." *Journal of World Trade* 28, no. 3 (June): 51–65.

Warren, Bill. 1980. *Imperialism: Pioneer of Capitalism.* London: Verso.

Wiarda, Howard J. 1996. *American Foreign Policy: Actors and Process.* New York: HarperCollins College Publishers.

Williams, William Appleman. 1972 *The Tragedy of American Diplomacy.* New Edition. New York: W. W. Norton and Company.

World Bank, The. 1987. *A World Bank Country Study: Korea, Managing the Industrial Transition.* Vols. 1 and 2. Washington, DC.

Yabuki, Susumu. 1995. *China's New Political Economy: The Giant Awakes.* Trans. Stephen M. Harner. Boulder, CO: Westview Press.

Yahuda, Michael. 1996. *The International Politics of the Asia-Pacific, 1945–1995.* London: Routledge.

Yuan, Gao. 1987. *Born Red: A Chronicle of the Cultural Revolution.* Stanford, CA: Stanford University Press.

Yunan Ribao. Various issues.

Zagoria, Donald S. 1993. "Clinton's Asia Policy." *Current History* 92, no.578 (December): 401–405.

Zhao, Quansheng. 1996. *Interpreting Chinese Foreign Policy*. Hong Kong: Oxford University Press.

Index

DATE DUE

Trexler Library
Muhlenberg College
Allentown, PA 18104

DEMCO